Indianola and Matagorda Island

1837-1887

A local history and visitor's guide for
a lost seaport and a barrier island on
the Texas Gulf Coast

by

Linda Wolff

EAKIN PRESS ✪ Austin, Texas

FIRST EDITION

Copyright © 1999
By Linda Wolff

Published in the United States of America
By Eakin Press
A Division of Sunbelt Media, Inc.
P.O. Drawer 90159 ▱ Austin, Texas 78709-0159
email: eakinpub@sig.net
▱ website: www.eakinpress.com ▱

ALL RIGHTS RESERVED

2 3 4 5 6 7 8 9

ISBN 1-57168-340-2

www.indianolabulletin.com

Library of Congress Cataloging-in-Publication Data

Wolff, Linda, 1947–
    Indianola and Matagorda Island, 1837–1887 : a local history and visitor's
guide for a lost seaport and a barrier island on the Texas Gulf Coast / by Linda
Wolff.
        p.   cm.
    Includes bibliographical references and index.
    ISBN 1-57168-340-2 (alk. paper)
    1. Indianola (Tex.)—History. 2. Matagorda Island (Tex.)—History. 3.
Indianola (Tex.) Guidebooks. 4. Matagorda Island (Tex.) Guidebooks. 5.
Indianola (Tex.)—Genealogy. 6. Matagorda Island (Tex.)—Genealogy. I. Title.
    F394.I5W65   2000
    976.4'121--dc21   99-23559
                                                                                CIP

Cover map of Calhoun County, 1863,
courtesy of Texas General Land Office

Table of Contents

Indian Point in November 1848—also known as Karlshaven (Carl's Harbor) by German immigrants who were brought to Texas by Prince Carl of Solms-Braunfels, commissioner-general of the Adelsverein.
— Courtesy Institute of Texan Cultures, San Antonio

Illustrations

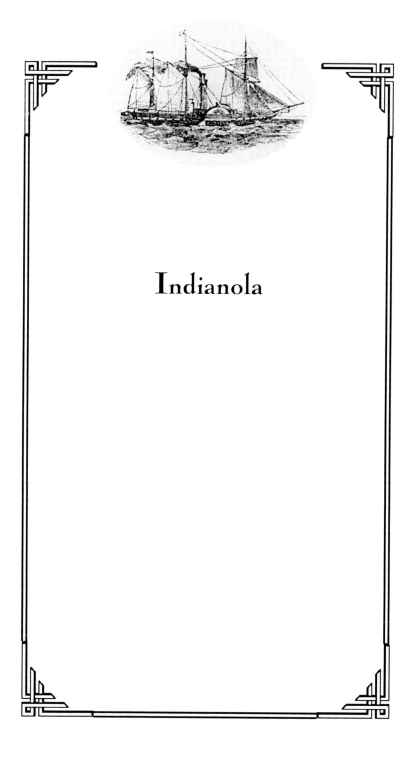

Indianola

Indianola Main Street, 1868.
— Courtesy Institute of Texan Cultures,
San Antonio

Old Town—Indianola

Galveston claimed the title the "Queen City," but her rival, Indianola, was known as the "Dream City of the Gulf." Like sisters they competed, each claiming to be the fairest of all.

There were differences between these two fair sister ports. Galveston was a port of commerce, but Indianola's future was tied to land grants in the Hill Country, forts on the Texas frontier, and efforts to establish trade with Mexico and even the Pacific Coast.

Through Indianola's portals poured immigrants, troops and military supplies, Jefferson Davis' camels, adventurers seeking a shorter route to the gold fields of California, merchants and politicians eager to establish themselves "where the action was." Ships leaving the port carried silver from Mexico for the U.S. Mint at New Orleans, beef hides, tins of turtle soup for diners in New York City, hides and then beef on the hoof, and eventually the first beef carcasses carried to another port under refrigeration.

Of the two sister seaports Indianola was the younger one. She began as Indian Point, a jut of land that marked the oyster reef dividing Matagorda Bay from Lavaca Bay.

In 1849 the seaport was renamed Indianola by Mrs. John Henry Brown, combining the word "Indian" with "*ola*," the Spanish word for wave. Not everyone was pleased with the name change. Many of the German immigrants continued to call it Karlshaven (Carl's Harbor) in honor of Prince Carl of Solms-Braunfels, who had brought them to Texas.

When Henry Morgan built a long wharf two miles closer to Powderhorn Lake to take advantage of the deeper water there, other businesses and residents followed him. At first the newer settlement was known as "Powderhorn" or "Brown's Addition," because it was so heavily promoted by newspaper editor John Henry Brown. But when Brown was lured to Galveston the Powderhorn area began to assume the name of "Indianola," leaving the original townsite the title of "Old Town." And so it was that the name "Indianola" was used when the settlement at Powderhorn was incorporated on February 7, 1853.

Indianola's streets were soon bursting at the seams with wagon trains drawn by oxen and mules carrying goods to destinations on the Chihuahua Trail and to western forts. There were some who thought Indianola might overtake Galveston. All agreed that the competition would be won by the first seaport to build a railroad that could carry goods and passengers to the West Coast.

During the Civil War, Indianola's railroad bed was destroyed, while the one at Galveston was spared. Galveston thus had the advantage, but the race was not yet won. During Reconstruction the competition was renewed.

The Indianola Railroad was completed to Clark's Station, where it was linked with the Gulf, West Texas and Mexican Railway that linked Port Lavaca to Victoria. During its earliest days it is said that the Gulf, West Texas and Mexican Railway cars were pulled by sails and mules, but these were replaced with locomotives.

Indianola soon became even more prosperous. Gas lights were installed to light the Indianola business district. Social life included theatrical productions, concerts by the Indianola City Brass Band, moonlit sailing excursions. The railroad line was extended to Cuero and was halted there only because the entire nation suffered a financial panic in 1873.

Less than two years later, Indianola would be struck by a horrific storm on September 16, 1875. The port city was crowded at the time with visitors eager to view the trial of Bill Taylor for the murder of Billy Sutton on an Indianola wharf. After the 1875 storm, thousands moved their businesses and homes inland, but others tried to rebuild, only to suffer another storm in 1880 and then a third and final storm on August 20, 1886. The "Dream City of the Gulf" had become a nightmare.

After every one of these storms, Galveston residents generously sent aid to their sister port. But Galvestonians did not learn from Indianola's ill fate. More than 5,000 lives were lost at Galveston during the 1900 Storm.

Indianola suffered an early demise, but she lingers in history as the "Dream City of the Gulf."

In the beginning . . .

1837—Two steamers are operating on Matagorda Bay. The steamer *Amite* serves ports on the bay and the steamer *Convoy*, owned by Capt. John D. Brower, runs to New Orleans. Other ships that call at Lavaca are the *Good Hope*, W.F. Hastings, master; *Martha*, William Watts, master; and the *Liberty*, Captain Haywood.

November 1837—During and immediately following the Texas Revolution, a series of seven military camps are established above Lavaca Bay. The seventh and final one is transferred from Cox's Point to Indian Point for a short time before it is abandoned. It is named Camp Chambers in honor of Thomas Jefferson Chambers.

1838—Earliest known passenger list for Lavaca records the arrival of eight passengers aboard the *Sarah Hughes* on Christmas Day. Goods are also landed by the *Wanderer*, *Marmion*, *Excel*, *Henry*, *Trapnell*, *Louisiana*, *Helen*, *Magnum Bonumo*, *Henry Flagg*, *Star*, and the *Good Hope*.

August 12, 1838—Thirty-three Gonzales Rangers, a volunteer group, and Joseph S. Martin lay out a townsite in Gonzales County which they name Walnut Springs. Six months later it will be renamed Seguin for Juan N. Seguin. Within a decade it will become a trade center and stopping point along the route taken by German immigrants to the Hill Country.

1839—Passengers arrive at Lavaca aboard the *Champion*, brig

Sam Houston, and schooners *Louisiana, Sarah, Amazon, Henry, Maria*, and *Martha*. Among these arrivals is Cesar Monod, who in 1849 will build a home in Castroville that is now the Landmark Inn.

January 21, 1839—Republic of Texas requires the secretary of state to acquire a section of land on the upper portion of Matagorda Island to be surveyed as a seaport. Sponsors of the bill anticipate that such a seaport would open vast stretches of West Texas to immigration. Populating West Texas, they believe, would lead to more trade and revenue for the penniless Republic.

The proposed seaport is named Port Calhoun and is surveyed at the site of Fort Washington, built during the Texas War for Independence. Alexander Somervell, a San Jacinto veteran, is named as its custom agent.

1840—Samuel Addison White, a resident of Texana and later to become a pioneer developer of Indian Point, creates a new breed of horse known as the "Texian" by breeding eighty selected fine Mexican mares foaled by a son of the famous *Leviathan* of Tennessee. The mares are bred to a stallion named simply *S.A. White's Stallion*.

A colt owned by S. A. White and sired by *Leviathan* is named for the town in Jackson County that White surveyed in 1830, Texana.

Leviathan was owned by the king of England until 1829, when the famous stallion was injured. An American purchased the stallion and brought him to Tennessee in 1830.

April 30, 1840—*The Morning Star* newspaper reports that "large numbers of English and German immigrants have come during the spring and are still coming into that part of the country." It is believed that these immigrants were all bound for Cat Spring, Industry, and Frelsburg, inspired by the letter written by Fredrich Ernst to friends in Oldenburg and Westphalia, Germany. The letters are subsequently published by a number of German newspapers.

August 8, 1840—Comanches attack Linnville. Most of the

town's residents are able to escape by fleeing to a ship in the bay, but the town is demolished. Eventually, a second settlement will arise closer to the bay that will become Lavaca, now known as Port Lavaca.

September 21, 1840—The firm of Ferguson and Harrell begins weekly passenger and freight service with the little paddlewheel steamer *Swan* between Texana and Decrow's Point on Matagorda Peninsula.

Passengers and freight are transferred to the few ships that ply the western Gulf of Mexico. Port Calhoun fails to attract any interest.

1842—Land acquired by Samuel Addison White at Indian Point by virtue of Headright Certificate No. 37 issued by Jackson County is surveyed, and White builds his home there.

February 5, 1842—Peters Colony Bill is approved by Republic of Texas Congress authorizing President Sam Houston to sign contracts with empresarios who will bring colonists to Texas in exchange for land.

February 15, 1842—Henri Castro of France obtains a contract to settle 600 immigrants in Texas with an option to increase that number to 1,000; however, all must be in Texas within three years, one-third within the first year. Initially Castro recruits from an office in Paris.

April 20, 1842—The *Mainzer Adelsverein at Biebrich am Rhein* (Society of Nobles for the Protection of German Immigrants in Texas) is organized to ease political and economic tensions in Germany. Land is to be purchased by the *Adelsverein* or secured as grants from the Republic of Texas. Each head of household is required to deposit with the *Adelsverein* 600 gulden (about $240) and each single person 300 gulden. Half of that amount is to be used for transportation to the colony and to provide housing when they arrive at the colony. The balance is to be held as a credit upon which the immigrants can draw for tools, farming equipment, and food rations until they secure their first harvest.

November 4, 1842—Alexander Somervell, customs agent on

Matagorda Island, answers a call from President Sam Houston to mount a full-scale expedition in the direction of the Rio Grande. Somervell meets 1,200 volunteer and drafted men waiting for his command at San Antonio.

December 7, 1842—Somervell and his men sweep into Laredo with little resistance. Some of the men plunder and loot the town. Somervell forces them to return the booty to the owners. Seeking military combat, he crosses the Rio Grande and approaches the Mexican village of Guerrero with 500 men and engages a few Mexican troops.

December 19, 1842—Somervell orders his troops home; however, five captains and their men refuse to obey the order. These continue onto Mier under the command of William S. Fisher. The day after Christmas they are forced to surrender and are marched to Matamoros. From there they will be marched 275 miles to Monterrey and then on to Saltillo.

New Year's Day, 1843—Henri Castro's first colonists arrive at Galveston aboard the *Ebro* but are not allowed to disembark until January 9. Within a week they are transferred to another vessel that takes them to Lavaca Bay, and from there they proceed overland to San Antonio.

At San Antonio they are halted and forced to take shelter in abandoned buildings because the Texas Rangers are not prepared to protect them from Indian depredations on their land grants, which lie thirty miles west of San Antonio.

1843—Charles Eckhardt, future co-founder of Yorktown, is a commission agent at Indianola.

February 11, 1843—Prisoners taken during the Mier Expedition escape from confinement at Hacienda de Salado. Many die, due to lack of food and water and exposure to the cold. The 176 survivors are rounded up by Mexican cavalry. Only four avoid capture and successfully return to Texas.

March 25, 1843—Mier Expedition survivors captured after their escape from Hacienda de Salado are forced to draw beans to determine who will be shot. The remaining prisoners are taken to the castle of Perote, where they are incarcerated with Woll's prisoners from San Antonio and the survivors of the Santa Fe Expedition.

April 1843—Samuel Augustus Maverick of San Antonio is released from the Perote prison through the intervention of United States Minister to Mexico Waddy Thompson. Maverick was taken prisoner by Mexican General Adrian Woll in San Antonio. In 1844 he will move his family to Decrow's Point on Matagorda Peninsula.

Fall 1843—Henri Castro begins to recruit more heavily from Alsace, Baden, Nassau, and Switzerland, where there are more farmers than in Paris. The *Jean Key* departs Antwerp on October 23, 1843, and the *Heinrich* a month later. Both are bound for Galveston and then Lavaca Bay. Castro is convinced that his colonization effort will make him a wealthy man. Neither he nor his competitors foresee the troubles that will befall them.

December 7, 1843—Among those aboard the *Heinrich* as it departs for Galveston are Nicholas Haby and Peter Bluntzer. Haby will become one of the great founders of Castroville. Bluntzer will develop Upper Meyersville by inspiring almost 200 people from three villages of the Upper Thur Valley in Alsace to immigrate to Texas during the 1850s.

April 9, 1844—Even more of Henri Castro's colonists depart Antwerp for Texas, these aboard the *Ocean*. They are recruited from the German states, Holland, and the French Provence of Alsace.

April 11, 1844—The *Heinrich* arrives at Galveston and the Henri Castro colonists are transferred to a small schooner or steamer bound for Lavaca Bay.

Late April 1844—Alsatian immigrant Peter Bluntzer is halted on his trek to Castroville because the spokes on a wagon wheel break as he is crossing the Guadalupe River. The wagon is overturned and his wife's hip is injured. After a stay in Victoria, Bluntzer purchases a tract of land on Coleto Creek from John Pettus, an Austin colonist. There he develops "Upper Meyersville" with immigrants he brings from the Upper Thur Valley between 1857 and 1860.

May 1844—Prince Carl of Solms-Braunfels is appointed commissioner general by the *Adelsverein* for its projected colony, and he sails for Texas.

May 12, 1844—Another group of Henri Castro's colonists depart Antwerp for Texas, these aboard the *Jeanette Marie*. Nearly all of the group are from Alsace.

May 19, 1844—Henri Castro and Prince Carl of Solms-Braunfels, accompanied by another empresario, Bourgeois d'Orvanne, all depart for Texas aboard the steamship *Caledonia*. At New Orleans, Castro suggests to Prince Carl and d'Orvanne that they all work cooperatively, but his offer is rebuffed.

May 29, 1844—*Northern Standard* reports "a large number of French and German emigrants have lately arrived from the United States and settled near Victoria, and it is believed that great numbers of emigrants from Europe will remove to that section come Autumn."

July 1844—The first of the *Adelsverein* immigrants arrive in Galveston aboard the *Weser*. Prince Carl is unprepared when they arrive.

Seeking a suitable port, the prince describes Lavaca (now Port Lavaca) as a town of four houses. He decides on Indian Point below Gallinipper Point where the water is deeper. An agreement is struck with Samuel Addison White, who holds title to the land at Indian Point. Among the Germans the port is known as *Karlshaven* (Carl's Harbor).

July 19, 1844—Henri Castro meets with his colonists stalled in San Antonio and assures them that they will soon be able to take possession of their lands on the Medina River. He departs with five members of Capt. Jack Hays' Ranger Company and John James, deputy surveyor for Bexar County, to inspect his land grant.

July 31, 1844—Henri Castro returns to his colonists still stalled at San Antonio and becomes furious when he learns that many of his colonists waiting there have been persuaded by agents for Prince Carl to settle in his colony instead.

September 2, 1844—The first of Henri Castro's colonists arrive on the banks of the Medina River to establish present-day Castroville.

September 16, 1844—The last of the Mier Expedition men held by Santa Anna at the Perote prison near Mexico City are released. Many have died in captivity from wounds, disease, and starvation. Some were able to escape by tunneling out of the prison or by bribing guards. A few were released by request of the U.S. and other foreign country officials. Among those who died in captivity were William H. Van Horn. During the Civil War, a home guard unit at Indianola will be named in his honor.

November 13, 1844—*Northern Standard* reports that four English and German vessels left Bremen for Galveston "several weeks since" with 250 families intended to settle in the colony of Colonel Fisher. About 2,000 more are awaiting passage, and vessels have since been chartered for their conveyance.

November 23, 1844—A second load of *Adelsverein* immigrants arrive in Galveston, these being aboard the brig *Johann Dethardt*. After a brief layover, the ship continues on to Lavaca Bay.

December 17, 1844—Prince Carl of Solms-Braunfels reaches an agreement with Samuel Addison White to purchase a landing site for the *Adelsverein* immigrants. He lays out a 152-mile route from Indian Point to New Braunfels by way of Agua Dulce near Bloomington, Victoria, Gonzales, and Seguin.

December 1844—The arrival of the brig *Johann Dethardt* at Galveston is followed by more ships bearing *Adelsverein* immigrants: the *Herrscel* on December 8, the *Ferdinand* on December 14, and the *Apollo*, arriving at Indian Point just before Christmas. Temporary shelters are erected on the beach.

Christmas Eve, 1844—At Prince Carl's invitation, the Rev. Louis Ervendberg, Texas' first German Protestant minister, welcomes the immigrants. A Christmas tree is decorated, carols are sung, and gifts are presented to the small children on Christmas Eve. On Christmas Day the Reverend Ervendberg conducts the first Holy Communion service at Indian Point.

1845—In a tent at Indian Point, Henry and Herman Runge, brothers, establish the H. Runge & Company Bank. Their bank will later be housed in one of only two stone buildings at Indianola.

February 3, 1845—Republic of Texas sets aside $1,500 for the purchase of land at Port Calhoun on Matagorda Island for a tower and "the necessary apparatus of a light."

March 21, 1845—The *Adelsverein's* first immigrants arrive at Las Fontanas (now Comal Springs) as the Spanish knew them. They lay out and name their new community "New Braunfels" in honor of Prince Carl's birthplace.

April 1845—Prince Carl departs New Braunfels without notice, leaving the immigrants there and those who will arrive later in the hands of Baron Otfried Hans Freiherr von Meusebach (John O. Meusebach), appointed commissioner general by the *Adelsverein* on February 24, 1845.

April 7, 1845—Hermann Seele departs Indianola with his friend, Heinrich Herbst. They walk most of the way to New Braunfels behind ox-driven wagons arriving a month later. Seele will be appointed by the Rev. Louis C. Ervenberg in August of 1845 to serve as New Braunfels' first schoolteacher. He teaches fifteen students under the shade of elm trees at the foot of Sophienburg Hill.

June 7, 1845—The *Northern Standard* reports that 125 passengers aboard the *Johans Dethard Sudering* arrived at Galveston from Breman and are bound for the *Adelsverein* Colony. Some of these boarded the sloop *Denmark* for Port Lavaca as they were destined for the Comal settlement "a few miles above Seguin on the Guadalupe."

August 11, 1845—William M. Cook acquires half interest in the land owned by Samuel Addison White at Indian Point.

A delegation of Mexican officials asks President Zachary Taylor to withdraw his troops to the Nueces River until the boundary dispute between Mexico and the United States can be resolved. Taylor refuses.

November 30, 1845—John O. Meusebach learns that 4,000 more immigrants are on their way to Indian Point and that a credit of only $24,000 has been opened with a New Orleans banker. By spring of 1846 more than 5,000 immigrants will arrive. Their situation will soon be desperate.

Late 1845—Heinrich Huck, a New Orleans merchant, learns that thousands of immigrants are camped on the beach at Indian Point unable to build even crude shelters because they have no lumber. He fills a schooner to capacity with large stores of lumber and medicine and sails to Indian Point to establish a lumberyard.

December 1845—Dr. Joseph Martin Reuss reaches Texas from his native Munnerstadt, Bavaria. He meets his future wife, Anna Gesine Stubbeman, working as a maid at the Tremont Hotel in Galveston. They marry after a whirlwind courtship, then sail for Indian Point.

Reuss and Heinrich Huck provide free medication and lumber for coffins to Germans suffering privations at Indian Point. Hundreds die of typhoid, cholera, or cerebro-spinal meningitis and are buried in unmarked, mass graves.

December 1845—Valentine Hoch, a stone mason, is among German immigrants who sail from the port of Bremen on the ship *Everhard* to Galveston. There he boards a smaller ship bound for Indianola. In 1857 he will build a home of sandstone at Hochheim and it will be used as a stage stop. (The home is still standing today.)

1846—Brown's Addition at Powderhorn Bayou is surveyed by

William Carl August Thielepape. At the same time he also surveys a railroad route between Powderhorn and Chocolate bayous. During this same period George Thielepape surveys the lots, blocks, and streets of Indian Point.

January 1846—More than 3,000 immigrants will have landed at Indian Point. Many are unable to make the trek inland to their land grants and they remain at Indian Point. They purchase land from Samuel Addison White.

February 19, 1846—The Republic of Texas becomes the twenty-eighth state of the United States of America.

March 1846—John O. Meusebach makes arrangements with the Torrey brothers, then of Houston, to move the immigrants and their belongings to their land grants near New Braunfels. About 100 teams arrive, but the wagons soon become mired up to their axles in mud on the rain-soaked prairies.

April 4, 1846—Calhoun County is created out of portions of Victoria, Jackson, and Matagorda counties.

April 11, 1846—Mexican Gen. Pedro de Ampudia, at Matamoros demands that Brevet Brigadier Gen. Zachary Taylor retreat to the Nueces River until the boundary dispute between Mexico and the United States can be resolved. Taylor refuses.

April 24, 1846—Mexican President Mariano Paredes declares "from this day defensive war begins." In Texas all available draft animals, cattle, and vehicles are bought up by the U.S. Army.

May 8, 1846—Fredericksburg is founded and named after Prince Frederick of Prussia, who is a member of the *Adelsverein.*

In Victoria the first issue of the *Texian Advocate* is published on a hand press. Printing equipment has been brought by water and ox-cart to Victoria by Thomas Sterne and John D. Logan from Van Buren, Arkansas. The newspaper carries news and advertising from Indian Point, and later Indianola.

American troops clash with the Mexican army at Palo Alto and four days later at Resaca de las Palmas. A special edition of the *Texian Advocate* in Victoria brings the news to residents of the Indian Point area.

June 26, 1846—*Northern Standard* newspaper at Clarksville reports that Col. L. P. Cooke while crossing the Guadalupe

River near Victoria "lost his horse, arms and money and, in this condition was found and killed by Caranchua Indians." The immigrants often form their own ranger companies to protect their settlements from Indian depredations.

Summer 1846—By some estimates, a thousand immigrants stranded on the coast die due to disease, inadequate shelter, and lack of food. Many perish on the road to their land grants. Those who make it to New Braunfels arrive sick and miserable.

August 2, 1846—Gen. John E. Wool disembarks at Lavaca from New Orleans with 2,500 "semi-trained, undisciplined, often insubordinate volunteers from the Middle West," bound for San Antonio. Many contract mumps, measles, and scarlet fever and die. More than 500 German immigrants at Indian Point (Karlshaven) are recruited as replacements by Capt. August C. Buchel.

September 13, 1846—Capt. Robert E. Lee, U.S. topographical engineer, spends his first night in Texas as a guest of Cesar Monod in Lavaca. By October he will have supervised the construction of a road that will be used by Gen. John E. Wool during an invasion of Mexico, forty miles below Eagle Pass, near the Presidio San Juan de Baptista.

November 1, 1846—Another shipload of settlers for the *Adelsverein* departs Hamburg for Texas aboard the *Albatross*. Among the passengers is H.L. Kreische, a native of Saxony, who will later build the Kreische Brewery on a bluff overlooking LaGrange.

November 21, 1846—Henri Castro signs a contract with James Power to land his colonists at Copano Bay rather than at Indian Point in an effort to reduce the exposure of his colonists to agents representing the *Adelsverein*. Castro fears that he will lose colonists that he has transported to Texas, but the agreement is never consummated.

March 3, 1847—The U.S. Congress authorizes $30,000 for the construction of two lighthouses, one at Galveston (Bolivar Point) and the other at Pass Cavallo (Matagorda Island).

April 16, 1847—Angelina Belle Peyton Eberly, heroine of the Archives War in Austin, leases a tavern, house, and lots in Port Lavaca from Edward Clegg. A year later she will open the American Hotel at Indian Point.

May 9, 1947—John O. Meusebach, commissioner-general for the *Adelsverein* and successor to Prince Carl of Solms-Braunfels, negotiates a treaty with the Comanches. Two months later he will resign, considering his work for the *Adelsverein* complete.

September 1847—Harrison and McCulloch establish the United States Stage Line, offering coach service from Port Lavaca to New Braunfels via Victoria, Cuero, Gonzales, and Seguin.

September 7, 1847—A post office is established at Indian Point with John W. Pope as postmaster.

October 1847—Samuel A. Maverick moves his family from Decrow's Point on Matagorda Peninsula to San Antonio and leaves a small herd of cattle on Matagorda Peninsula that he has reluctantly accepted as payment for a $1,200 loan. They are allowed to run free and have no brands. Residents soon refer to any cow without a brand as "one of Maverick's."

October 28, 1847—Margaret Evangeline Peyton, daughter and only surviving child of Angelina Eberly (heroine of the Archives War), is married to Port Lavaca attorney James T. Lytle, who is also a former Texas Ranger.

November 22, 1847—Congress authorizes the purchase of 2.5 acres of land on Matagorda Island from Thomas Jefferson Chambers overlooking Pass Cavallo at Calhoun for the erection of a lighthouse and keeper's residence. The purchase price is $250.

December 6, 1847—The brig *Matagorda* inaugurates service between New York City, Indianola, and other ports on the Gulf of Mexico.

December 17, 1847—James L. Allen, "the last messenger from

John O. Meusebach negotiated a treaty with ten Comanche chiefs that opened three million acres of Texas Hill Country to settlement. A bronze memorial depicting this event is located at Fredericksburg.
—Courtesy Henry Wolff, Jr.

the Alamo," advertises his hotel at Indian Point. He will later serve as Indianola's mayor and also as tax assessor and collec-tor for Calhoun County during the Civil War. In 1867 he will move to Hochheim.

1848—Seeing the success of J. B. Brown's coach service and how Indian Point and the Powderhorn areas are growing, Harrison and McCulloch add Indian Point to their route from the coast to New Braunfels.

The *Yacht* is run aground on Gallinipper Bar on each of her first seven voyages while her captains are trying to navigate their way to Port Lavaca. After extensive repairs are made, Charles Morgan decides to lengthen his wharf at Powderhorn so that his ships can dock there.

Sailing ships from Boston, New York, Philadelphia, Bal-timore, Pensacola, Mobile, New Orleans, and lesser Gulf ports crowd the four wharves at Indian Point. Ships commonly seen there include the *Ocean Wave, Harrison, Pennsylvania, Tom Paine, Montana, Sears, Mary Adeline, Matagorda, European, America,* and *Victoria.* Above-average service between Galveston and Indianola is provided by three schooners, the *European,* the *America,* and the *Adeline.*

Soon the U.S. Mail Steamship line will replace their sail lighters with a steam propeller lighter, the *Jerry Smith.* They also add two sidewheel steamers, the *Portland* and *Galveston,* to begin service from New Orleans to Indianola, touching only at Galveston.

Oleanders are introduced from the West Indies. They and the tamarisk are widely used as windbreaks.

1848 to 1854—The Texas General Land Office issues 3,492 certificates for the Fisher-Miller grant for the *Adelsverein* colonists and 558 for Castro's colonists.

Early 1848—Indian Point becomes a wholesale center, supplying merchants of inland towns (and military posts) with groceries, hardware, lumber, clothing, furniture, and other items in exchange for cotton, dry hides, tallow, and pecans. William M. Cook builds Indian Point's fourth wharf. The others were built by Samuel A. White, the *Adelsverein,* and Theodore Miller.

January 1848—Viktor Bracht, an explorer and merchant-author, who came to Texas in 1845, describes Matagorda Bay in his book as "just as extensive as Galveston Bay and much better suited for navigation."

Regular weekly stagecoach service is established between Victoria and Indianola by John B. Brown of Victoria. His stagecoaches meet the steamship *Yacht* owned by the New Orleans shipping firm of Harris and Morgan. The *Yacht* provides weekly service between Galveston and Port Lavaca with a stop at Indian Point.

January 6, 1848—A new ferry service across the Guadalupe River reduces the travel distance between Lavaca and Goliad by twenty miles. The crossing is sixteen miles from Lavaca and about the same distance from Victoria.

January 20, 1848—Theodore Miller becomes acting agent for the German Immigration Company which succeeds the bankrupt *Adelsverein*. Indian Point will continue to be the landing point for hundreds of Germans. The German Immigration Company is also identified as the Lavaca, Guadalupe, and San Saba Railroad Company.

February 2, 1848— Treaty of Guadalupe Hidalgo is signed ending the Mexican War and establishing Rio Grande as the boundary between the United States and Mexico.

ECKHARDT'S TRAIL

Completion of Eckhardt's route to the Hill Country shortened the immigrants' journey by twenty miles.
— From *Yorktown, Texas 150 Year Anniversary* by Yorktown Historical Society

February 7, 1848 —Charles Eckhardt, a prosperous merchant at Indianola, contracts with John A. King to survey and build a public road from Victoria to the prospective town of Yorktown and from there to New Braunfels. The distance to New Braunfels is reduced by twenty-six miles.

Eckhardt also becomes the prime exporter of wool from Saxon sheep brought through Indian Point for sheep raisers in the Fredericksburg area of the Hill Country. The Saxony sheep are crossed with the Merino sheep that were brought through Indian Point from Spain to be crossed with Mexican sheep. Eckhardt also ships native gama grass hay to Mobile, Alabama.

March 1848 —Indianola residents are interested in the new Bullard windmill but it soon proves to be useless at Indianola due to the intrusion of salt water into the sands underlying the coastal country. Residents will be forced for some time to rely on cisterns made of shell-crete to capture rain water.

April 1848—The *Advocate* reports that the steamer *Victoria* has come up the Guadalupe River as far as the Donaldson's place.

April 2, 1848—Charles Eckhardt and some friends purchase a tract of land from John York to establish a business, midway between Indianola and San Antonio. After his death in 1852, the business will be operated by his brother, Caesar, as C. Eckhardt & Sons.

May 12, 1848—The steamship *Maria Birta* arrives from Vera Cruz carrying Colonel Hays' regiment of Texas Volunteers who are then disbanded because the Mexican War has ended. Other homeward bound troops will return through the port throughout the summer.

June 1848—The *Advocate* reports that steamers are able to navigate the Guadalupe as far as the San Antonio River, at which point freight is transferred to keelboat to carry it to Goliad.

July 6, 1848—Samuel Addison White sells more than 100 town lots at Indian Point to "American" settlers. German residents are not enthusiastic about the sale as they are, with few exceptions, opposed to slavery.

July 9, 1848—Dr. Levi Jones, a Galveston physician, files legal documents with the county clerk in Port Lavaca to establish a commercial port to be known as LaSalle on the western shore of Matagorda Bay below Powderhorn Bayou and about six miles from Indian Point. In his promotional pamphlet Jones envisions a roadway from Matagorda Bay to the Pacific. Jones was active in the development of Galveston prior to his arrival in Calhoun County.

July 18, 1848—The Rev. Daniel Baker, D.D., a pioneer Presbyterian missionary, writes his son from Port Lavaca during a trip to visit Presbyterian congregations at Indian Point, Port Lavaca, Victoria, and Texana.

August 1848—*Texian Advocate* reports that a commercial wagon road is proposed from (Port) Lavaca via San Antonio to Chihuahua and California. Sam Maverick, the celebrated John C. "Jack" Hays, and thirty citizens will lay off the road.

September 14, 1848—German writer Gustav Dresel dies of yellow fever in Galveston after a short visit to Indianola, while serving as business manager for the *Adelsverein.* Dresel also served as the first German consul in Texas for Duke Adolph of Nassau.

September 28, 1848—The *Democratic Telegraph and Texas Register* reports on the burial of the remains of the Mier prisoners and those under Dawson's command on a bluff overlooking LaGrange. Four of the victims were from Victoria. The memorial is built on land purchased by H. L. Kreische, an immigrant through the Port of Indianola, for his home and brewery. Today the site is Monument Hill & Kreische Brewery State Historical Park.

November 7, 1848—The War Department orders Bvt. Maj. Jefferson Van Horne to establish a military post in the area of El Paso del Norte (El Paso). Supplies for this fort will pour through the Port of Indianola and it also becomes a major stop along what will become known as the Chihuahua Trail.

December 1848—James D. Cochran, H. H. Rogers, and Samuel Addison White open a beef canning plant on the outskirts of Indian Point, but it meets with only moderate success. Prior to this time only the leather and tallow were harvested from the beeves and the meat was left to rot on the prairie because there was no way to preserve it.

December 9, 1848—The U.S. government purchases five acres of land from Thomas Jefferson Chambers for $500 on Matagorda Island for the construction of a lighthouse. This is in addition to the two and a half acres that were purchased in November.

Late 1848-1849—Hundreds die in Lavaca and more than a thousand at Indianola from Asiatic cholera brought by ship from New Orleans. The January 1849 edition of the *Texian Advocate* includes a letter from Maj. Pitcairn Morrison, 8th Regiment, U.S. Infantry, thanking Port Lavaca residents who turned schools and churches into hospitals for his sick troops.

The regiment's commander, Gen. William Jenkins Worth, contracts the disease and will die on May 7, 1849, in San Antonio. (It is for him that Fort Worth is named.)

Cholera in San Antonio also claims the life of Henry M. Lewis and all of the editorial staff of his newspaper, the *West Texan*. Lewis was formerly a resident of Indianola.

1849—Port Lavaca increases its wharfage fees, an act that affirms Morgan's decision to move his operation to Powderhorn where the water is deeper.

James M. Foster, a wealthy Kentucky rancher, establishes holding pens for his cattle a couple miles west of Indianola on the northern shore of Powderhorn Lake. His wharf at Indianola extends to deep water on the bay. Foster contracts with Morgan Steamship for two steamers each week to take his cattle.

February 1, 1849—Indian Point is renamed Indianola as suggested by Mrs. (Mary) John Henry Brown, combining the word "Indian" from its original name with "*ola*," the Spanish word for wave. Some are unhappy with the name change, but her will prevails.

December 19, 1849—The bill granting the federal government full legal jurisdiction over the site purchased for the lighthouse is approved by the Texas Legislature but it will languish on the governor's desk for another two years unsigned.

December 21, 1849—Brig *Matagorda* departs New York City and encounters severe cold. Three weeks later when she arrives at Indianola several of her crew members "undergo amputation of frostbitten limbs."

1850s

1850 census—Angelina Belle Peyton Eberly, owner of the American Hotel, is the principal property holder in the bustling seaport of Indianola with assets valued at $50,000.

1850—Solomon G. Cunningham purchases J.M. Foster's livestock holding pens on Matagorda Bay. Foster has been shipping live cattle to New Orleans for at least a year.

The United States Congress approves $15,000 for the construction of a lighthouse on Matagorda Island, but two years will pass before it is built.

Nicholas Zink, an engineer for the *Adelsverein* and the surveyor for the City of New Braunfels, establishes Sisterdale about fifty miles northwest of San Antonio after having a falling out with Prince Carl of Solms-Braunfels.

Early 1850s—The Sulphur Spring settlement develops where the spring feeds into Ojo de Agua Creek, two miles northeast of present-day Runge in Karnes County, and is crossed by the road from Goliad to San Antonio. It will become a stagecoach stop for travelers from Indianola. Between 1859 and 1867, Sulphur Spring will become known as Mineral Spring.

January 25, 1850—*Texian Advocate* notes that immigrants are still pouring through the port at Indianola. Most are German, arriving from the ports of Bremen and Antwerp. By October, Capt. August C. Buchel will be appointed the agent of the German Immigration Company at Indianola.

February 1, 1850—Trade between Indianola, Santa Fe, and Chihuahua is opened with a train of eighteen wagons departing from Indianola for Santa Fe by way of Paso del Norte (El Paso).

February 10, 1850—The steamer *Telegraph* runs aground on Gallinipper Bar. A sudden norther drives the *Mary Somers* upon a reef as she is employed to remove the *Telegraph's* cargo. The same storm also drives the *Monterrey* onto Matagorda Island.

The Buffalo Bayou, Brazos and Colorado Railway is chartered by a group of Houston and Harrisburg businessmen to strengthen their position on Galveston Bay. They have become concerned that Indianola might control all traffic of goods bound for Austin and Central Texas.

March 2, 1850—Indianola celebrates Texas' Independence Day with a procession accompanied by band music to Mrs. Angelina Belle Peyton Eberly's hotel, where the Texas Declaration of Independence is read by John Henry Brown.

Late March 1850—A military road is opened from Indianola through Green Lake, Pierpont, Yorktown, and Sutherland Springs to San Antonio for the movement of military supplies and troops. The shorter route is now measured at ninety-five miles from the bay to San Antonio.

May 11, 1850—Masonic Lodge No. 84 is organized at Indianola. (After the storm of 1886, the lodge will be moved to Port Lavaca.)

May 31, 1850—Dr. Levi Jones sells lots in his LaSalle Addition in a public sale. The results are disappointing; however, he continues his promotion of the community, competing with Indianola.

June 1, 1850—LaSalle and El Paso Railway Company is chartered and promoted by Levi Jones but it will never be built.

June 16, 1850—Capt. Parker H. French brings a wagon train of 200 immigrants through (Port) Lavaca who have paid $250 each for a shorter route to the California gold fields that also bypasses the journey around Cape Horn.

July 1850—A squall in Matagorda Bay causes damage to the lighter *Jerry Smith* and the Guadalupe River steamers the *Envoy* and the *Palmetto,* all moored at Indianola. The schooner *Ann,* lying at LaSalle three miles below Indianola, is not damaged. She is the first ship to use the port there, discharging a cargo of 78,000 feet of lumber. The second ship to arrive at LaSalle will be the schooner *Aurora Borealis* on July 17 with 76,000 feet of lumber.

August 20, 1850—The U.S. Boundary Commission arrives to survey and mark the boundary between the United States and Mexico as mandated by the 1848 Treaty of Guadalupe Hidalgo. John Henry Brown's warehouse is emptied to give a dinner in honor of the commission. One of the commission's duties is to make observations to determine the feasibility of a railroad route from the Gulf of Mexico to the Pacific.

August 31, 1850—John Russell Bartlett arrives at Indianola as U.S. commissioner of the United States and Mexican Boundary Commission. In 1854 he will publish *Personal Narrative of Explorations and Incidents: In Texas, New Mexico, California, Sonora and Chihuahua, 1850-1853,* which becomes an "invaluable guidebook and reference work for the tide of immigration . . . as a result of the California gold discoveries."

September 5, 1850—The San Antonio and Mexican Gulf Railroad is chartered. The original plan is to build it from Saluria on Matagorda Island to San Antonio.

September 18, 1850—An expedition of gold seekers brought through the Port of Indianola by Parker French arrives at El Paso del Norte (El Paso). Three men have died and twenty continue on their own through Mexico. French manages to elude a government messenger from San Antonio bearing a warrant for his arrest.

October 1850—A wharf at Indianola is extended by Capt. John A. Rogers to a water depth of ten feet to meet the challenge posed by Levi Jones' wharf at LaSalle.

Seven vessels are running regularly between Mobile and Pensacola to Indianola to fill the demand for lumber in West

Texas. Weekly mail service between Indianola, Saluria, Corpus Christi, and Brownsville is provided by boat.

October 19, 1850—The schooner *Catherine Hall* sets a new record for speed of transit between New York City and Indianola: only fourteen days.

November 1850—*William Penn* is brought by Capt. J. O. Wheeler to supplement the *Kate Ward* in providing additional freight and passenger service on the Guadalupe River between Victoria and the bay.

November 30, 1850—The *Lavaca Commercial* reported that "Mr. Harris of Harris and Morgan of New Orleans killed a fine large panther one day last week at Sand Point."

About 1851—Carl Hilmar Guenther is among German immigrants arriving at Indianola. He trudges beside a provision wagon the ninety-five miles to San Antonio and then builds the first mill on Live Oak Creek nine miles west of Fredericksburg. (In 1859 he will build the first mill in San Antonio which will later be known as Pioneer Flour Mills.)

January 9, 1851—The *Palmetto* is run aground at Pass Cavallo. No lives are lost, but cargo and passenger baggage are ruined. Charles Morgan ends stops by his ships at Saluria on Matagorda Island.

February 1851—Indianola Presbyterian Church erects the first house of worship at Indianola. The building is also used by the community's other congregations.

February 13, 1851—The *Texian Advocate* announces that a new route is opened between Indianola and Victoria via Green Lake to avoid the mud wallows above and below Chocolate Creek.

March 1851—Saltmarsh Stage Line is transporting U.S. Mail from Indianola to San Antonio via Lavaca, McGrew's, Victoria, and Sulphur Springs. The schedule is tied to the arrival and departure of the Harris and Morgan steamships at Powderhorn.

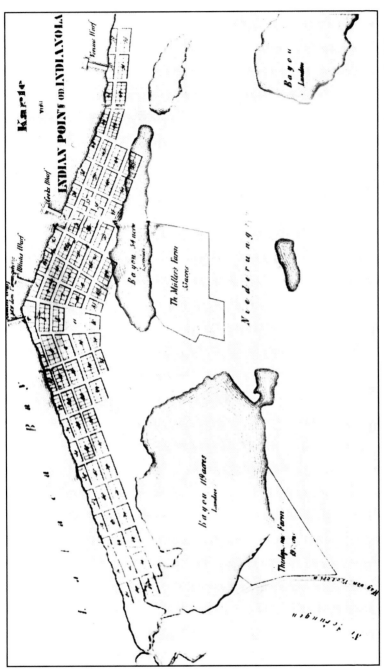

Map of Indian Point or Indianola, 1851. Four wharves can be seen and at far left, from old Town Lake, is marked the "Wey von Victoria."

— Courtesy Institute of Texan Cultures, San Antonio

April 1851—A train of 400 vehicles is filled with freight unloaded from the schooner *P.B. Savery* for Lewis, Groesbeck and Coons for the Chihuahua trade. The train includes heavy wagons, drawn by six mules or six or eight oxen, and *carettas*, the brightly painted two-wheeled Mexican carts pulled by four or six oxen.

June 1851—Steamship *Delta* makes first run up Guadalupe River, at less cost than moving the freight by wagon.

June 25, 1851—Summer storms inflict wind and water damage to every building at Saluria. Every wharf at Lavaca (now Port Lavaca) is destroyed. The *William Penn* is torn from her mooring at Old Town at Indian Point, driven toward shore and sunk in five feet of water. The *Mexico* is torn from her anchors and grounded on a bar in the bay. Vessels anchored in Powderhorn Bayou and Powderhorn Lake escape the storm's wrath. The steamship *Maria Birt* is lost in the Gulf but no lives are lost. Mail destined for Victoria, San Antonio, and West Texas is lost in the bay.

August 1851—Ice cut in New England is brought to Indianola. Casimer Villeneuve, owner of the Alhambra Hotel, loads a block of the ice into a heavy crate and then onto a cart. He sends it to the newsroom of the *Texian Advocate* at Victoria.

November 1851—John Huff begins to advertise the establishment of a resort hotel, Huff's Hotel, at Decrow's Point on Matagorda Peninsula, "an excellent place for fishing and bathing."

December 1851—River traffic on the Guadalupe River is halted because there is too much debris in the river and the bay. A survey by J. E. Park reports that it would cost $20,600 to clear the river as far as Seguin.

December 31, 1851—Gilbert Onderdonk arrives at Indianola and buys a horse that takes him to the Green Lake settlement where he is employed by the Rev. Stephen Cocke. He learns how to raise cattle, horses, and mules but will later achieve greater renown as a horticulturist specializing in fruits. (His nursery above Victoria becomes the present-day settlement of Nursery.)

1852—Indianola is revisited by a cholera epidemic and suffers its first yellow fever epidemic, brought in from the West Indies.

January 1852—Indianola gains its first newspaper, the *Indianola Bulletin*, with John Henry Brown as its publisher and editor. Brown was formerly associated with the *Texian Advocate* as a printer and editor, the *Texas Sentinel* in Austin, and with several newspapers in Missouri prior to his move to Texas.

February 1852—San Antonio, Seguin, Gonzales, Victoria, and Indianola Semi-Weekly Stage Service begins operation. The line is owned by J. L. Allen of Indianola, "the last messenger from the Alamo."

March 26, 1852—Six lives are lost when the steamship *Independence* capsizes in Pass Cavallo during a storm.

May 1852—The brig *Russell* with Capt. E. K. Cooper arrives with the prefabricated plates for the cast-iron lighthouse to be placed on Matagorda Island after having first discharged the parts for the Bolivar Point Lighthouse.

August 1852—Baldridge, Sparks and Co. begins construction of a new wharf near Powderhorn Bayou that is sixteen feet wide and 1,500 feet long with a warehouse large enough to dock five vessels.

August 21, 1852—Calhoun County seat is moved from Port Lavaca to Indianola at Powderhorn. Gradually Indian Point will become known as "Old Town."

September 1852—Casimer and Matilda Villeneuve purchase seven lots in Brown's Addition to erect a hotel, the Casimer House. The *Texian Advocate* reports that it will accommodate 150 overnight guests.

September 29, 1852—The tower for the Matagorda Island Lighthouse is complete, but the lighting apparatus will not be installed until Christmas.

Detail from 1852 of Indianola Bulletin. *Note rates for stage line, and that ox wagons are in demand. Attorney Stockdale will later be elected lieutenant governor and will serve, briefly, as governor of Texas in 1865 when Gov. Pendleton Murrah flees to Mexico with the fall of the Confederacy.*

— Courtesy Institute of Texan Cultures, San Antonio

November 15, 1852— Calhoun County Commissioners Court approves the construction of a roadway between Indi-anola, LaSalle, Alligator Head (now known as Port O'Con-nor), and Saluria on Matagorda Island.

H. W. Hawes is granted right to operate the ferries that span Pearce and McHenry bayous between Alligator Head on the mainland and Saluria on the island. A horse and rider are charged fifty cents.

December 31, 1852— Matagorda Island Lighthouse is lit by

Capt. James Cummings, its first keeper. It is the first tower to be lit on the Texas coast.

February 7, 1853—Incorporation of the City of Indianola is approved by the state legislature and the boundaries are set.

1853—Mrs. Henry Sheppard, wife of Capt. Henry Sheppard, hosts a dinner aboard the *Perseverance* while it is moored at an Indianola T-head. A fire breaks out and the dinner guests escape, but the vessel must be steamed out into the bay where it burns all night. (Later the bell will be salvaged and given to St. Mark's Lutheran Church in Cuero, where it remains.)

May 12, 1853—Judge William M. Varnell of Indianola, leading the Concho Expedition Company, arrives at noon in Gonzales. He is leading a group of gold seekers that includes many prominent residents of Calhoun County. They are en route to the San Saba region north of Austin, where it is said that there are gold veins as rich as any in California.

May 26, 1853—Bvt. Lt. Col. W. G. Freeman inspects U.S. Army depot being built at Indianola to receive military supplies bound for San Antonio and Austin. The depot includes five structures and a 250-foot-long wharf upon which is laid a railroad rail.

June 21, 1853—The Concho Expedition Company led by Judge William M. Varnell returns to Port Lavaca and Indianola empty-handed. The would-be miners report that they viewed some beautiful country, "but alas no gold." They were seeking gold along the San Saba River north of Austin.

July 27, 1853—A bucket brigade is unable to halt a fire that destroys four warehouses, lumber, and goods belonging to Baldridge, Sparks & Co.; the home of Thomas Rooke and his family on an upper floor; the office of Drs. Lewis & F. E. Hughes; and the home of Dr. Hughes on the upper floor.

September 1853—More yellow fever cases are reported, prompting an exodus from Indian Point to Powderhorn. Houses and business buildings are moved alike. Some are rolled on logs or multiple sets of wheels. At least one building, owned by William M. Varnell, is simply pushed into the bay and floated to its new location at Powderhorn.

September 23, 1853—Thomas Sterne, co-owner of the *Texian Advocate* newspaper in Victoria, sells his interest to George W. Palmer. Within months John D. Logan sells his interest to John J. Jamieson, who also sells to Palmer.

1854—The first Lutheran church is formally organized at Indianola. As early as 1848, a Victoria and Indian Point German mission was led by Henry Bauer.

The Indianola *Saengerbund*, an Indianola singing group, travels to San Antonio to participate in the second annual *Saengerfest*.

January 25, 1854—Alexander Somervell, one of Saluria's three founders, departs from Lavaca on a boat bound for Matagorda Island with a large amount of money secured around his waist. Later the boat is found capsized. Somervell is lashed to the timbers of his boat and the money is gone.

In 1842, under orders from President Sam Houston, Somervell led a punitive raid into Mexico. He later ordered the men to disband. Those who refused were organized by William S. Fisher into the Mier Expedition, which led to the famous "Draw of the Black Bean" incident. In December of 1842 Somervell was appointed the collector of customs for the Calhoun District which includes Matagorda Island, a position he held until his mysterious death.

Spring 1854—The Matagorda Island Lighthouse gets its first paint job of white, red, and black bands. Within a few months a summer storm damages the lantern, the light's reflectors, and the keeper's house.

April 24, 1854—The town of Comfort is established by deeds recorded in Bexar County by founder-surveyor Herman Altgelt, who had immigrated through the Port of Indianola only months earlier.

September 1854—John Henry Brown of Indianola departs for Galveston; publication of the *Indianola Bulletin* is suspended.

September 18, 1854—A storm strikes the upper Texas coast, wrecking every vessel in Matagorda Bay and the wharves at Indianola. There is also much damage at (Port) Lavaca but less at Powderhorn and at LaSalle, below Powderhorn Lake. The storm is followed by another yellow fever epidemic.

December 3, 1854—The first of the Polish immigrants from Upper Silesia arrive at Galveston aboard the bark *Weser*. More arrive a few days later aboard the brig *Antoinette*. With only a few ox-drawn carts to carry their possessions they walk from Galveston to Indianola and then to the junction of the San Antonio and Cibolo rivers to establish Panna Maria. With them they bring a cross from their parish church.

December 24, 1854—Father Leopold Moczygemba and the first of Polish immigrants from Upper Silesia celebrate their first mass at the junction of the San Antonio and Cibolo rivers. The location becomes the site of the Church of the Immaculate Conception at Panna Maria.

February 1855—A second group of Polish immigrants to Texas is met at Indianola by Charles de Montel, who escorts them to San Antonio by ox-cart. They join the John James project to populate the town of Bandera, which he has platted on the Medina River.

March 3, 1855—Congress appropriates $30,000 for the purchase of camels and authorizes them to be imported to determine if they can be used to haul military supplies to forts that are strung across West Texas and the Southwest to California.

Capt. Robert E. Lee is promoted to lieutenant colonel, Second U.S. Cavalry.

Spring 1855—Andrew Marschalk, Sr., revives publication of *Indianola Bulletin*.

Drought causes lower end of Stevens Bayou to dry up. Water is so scarce that a glass of rain water costs more than a stein of beer (five cents).

May 5, 1855 —Dr. William D. Kelly urges the Indianola City Council to establish a city hospital to treat those stricken with yellow fever. On May 21 the council approves the establishment of a hospital and a board of health.

May 21, 1855—Calhoun County Commissioners Court grants James McCoppin the right to establish a ferry across Powderhorn Bayou.

June 1855—The Indianola City Aldermen pass an ordinance banning anyone from keeping a house of ill-fame within the city limits or to allow a structure to be used as a bawdy house.

August 1855—W. H. Woodward purchases an interest in *Indianola Bulletin* and Marschalk is succeeded by his son, A. M. Marschalk, Jr.

Late 1855—Joseph M. Bickford, a graduate of Dartmouth College, opens a school on Matagorda Island.

December 15, 1855—Another group of Polish immigrants arrives at Panna Maria following the same route as the first group, from Galveston to Indianola, and then inland. Most settle at Panna Maria, but thirteen familes proceed to Martinez where they from the colony of St. Hedwig.

1856—Construction begins on the bed for the San Antonio and Mexican Gulf Railroad, from Port Lavaca to Clark Station, a distance of five miles.

Gohmert's Theater is built at Yorktown in 1856 with a large dance hall and a stage with curtains and scenery. Stage performances there become so popular that Indianola and San Antonio teamsters schedule their arrivals at Yorktown to see them. The first performance is *Einer muss Hieraten*.

April 29, 1856—The naval store ship *Supply* enters Matagorda Bay through Pass Cavallo with the camels that the U.S. Army will use to determine if camels can be used to transport military supplies. Unfortunately, the swells in the bay are so great that the camels cannot be transferred onto the *Fashion* so that they can be unloaded at the wharf at Indianola. The *Supply* and the *Fashion* return to the mouth of the Mississippi, where the transfer is made to the more shallow draft boat.

May 14, 1856—At last, thirty-four camels are unloaded onto a wharf at Indianola. The entire town turns out to see them. Decorated with red blankets, the camels are led by their

Arabian handlers to a ten-acre corral built behind Old Town (now Magnolia Beach). Fencing material is in short supply so prickly pear is used as a substitute; however, the camels soon eat the prickly pear fence built to contain them. Horses fear the camels, but oxen are unaffected.

June 4, 1856—Light loads are placed on the camels and they begin their westward trek. They will arrive in Victoria on June 8, at San Antonio on June 18, and at their destination, Camp Verde, on August 26, 1856.

August 12, 1856—A pair of socks knitted by Mrs. Mary A. Shirkey of Victoria from camel fleece is presented to President Franklin Pierce. Pierce returns the favor by sending her a silver goblet.

September 1, 1856—The state legislature charters the Powderhorn, Victoria and Gonzales Railroad Company, but sufficient capital cannot be raised.

September 26, 1856—Polish immigrants complete the Church of the Immaculate Conception at Panna Maria in Karnes County and install the cross brought from their Upper Silesia parish church in 1854.

October 8, 1856—Western Texas Wharf Company is organized at Indianola to erect a new long wharf at Powderhorn to accommodate Southern Steamship Company vessels, as Harris and Morgan are then known.

October 16, 1856—A private shipment of camels arrives at Galveston consigned to a Mrs. Thomas Watson. Galveston authorities boarding the ship are convinced that the camels are only a cover for a shipload of slaves that were unloaded somewhere else on the Texas Gulf Coast.

Ultimately, the camels are purchased by Lieutenant Governor F. R. Lubbock, who places them on his ranch on Sim's Bayou.

Likewise, a separate ship of camels arrives at Indian Point from the Canary Islands accompanied by Juan Gonzales, a Canary Island native, and Joseph Mendez of Madrid, Spain.

They are consigned to "the widow Watson," who refuses to accept them. Penniless and with no means to return to their homelands, Gonzales and Mendez settle at Indian Point, where they marry and become highly regarded citizens. (They are buried in the Zimmerman Cemetery.)

Late 1856—Another group of Polish Immigrants—about thirty families—arrives at Panna Maria. These and earlier arrivals establish parish comunities in San Antonio, St. Hedwig, Falls City, Kosciusko, Hobson, Runge, Meyersville, Cestohowa, Polaski, Orange Grove, and McCook. Others will settle at Victoria, Yorktown, Karnes City, and Helena.

November 25, 1856—Maj. Henry C. Wayne sends twenty-five camels from Camp Verde to San Antonio through Castroville to determine their usefulness as pack animals.

Christmas 1856—A typical Christmas feast includes a jug of whiskey purchased for fifty cents, firecrackers for the children, taffy pulled from molasses, wild turkey, wild hog, and possum served with sweet potatoes and corn cakes wrapped in a corn shuck and baked in the fire's hot ashes.

1857—Hugh Walker Hawes sells a fifty-foot square of land on the north side of McHenry Bayou to the U.S. government for the construction of the Saluria Light.

Ice arrives by wagons in San Antonio from Indianola. A glass of whiskey is five cents plain, or fifteen cents with ice.

January 1857—Cornelius Vanderbilt places the steamship *Daniel Webster* into service between New York and Indianola to spite his rival, Charles Morgan.

January 24, 1857—C. A. Ogsbury halts publication of *Indianola Bulletin*, but he will resume its publication in 1866.

January 29, 1857—Forty-one camels arrive at Indianola aboard the *Suwanee*, after being unloaded from the store ship *Supply*.

March 19, 1857—Lt. Col. Robert E. Lee, Second U.S. Cavalry, is again a guest of the Cesar Monod family. For the next ten days he will conduct a military court at Indianola. He will find time on March 27 to write to his youngest daughter.

May 17, 1857—In two hours a "blue norther" freezes the bay twenty feet from shore.

May 31, 1857—A Harris and Morgan steamship, the *Louisiana*, with Capt. Henry Sheppard in command, catches fire five miles out from the port at Galveston. Thirty-five lives are lost.

June 1857—Alfred P. Bennett establishes the *Indianolian* newspaper.

The U.S. Post Office signs a contract with James E. Birch of Swansea, Massachusetts, for twice-monthly mail service between San Antonio and San Diego. Coaches from Indianola meeting this line provide the first Gulf of Mexico to California passenger service.

June 4, 1857—Major Wayne departs Indianola with forty-one camels bound for Camp Verde, the second and final installment. They will arrive in San Antonio on June 19, 1857.

September 5, 1857—D. M. Stapp succeeds Dr. Levi Jones as collector of customs for the District of Saluria.

September 11, 1857—James E. Birch, who has just signed a contract to provide mail service between San Antonio and San Diego, is among 421 passengers who lose their lives aboard the *Central America* when the ship encounters a hurricane off the Florida coast. His widow sells his share to O. H. Kelton of Charleston, South Carolina.

1858—Polish settlers from Karnes County who had arrived in 1855 move again, this time to "Gazeta" (Garcitas) near the point where Garcitas Creek empties into Lavaca Bay on the Spanish land grant of Valentin Garcia. After the 1886 storm, they will rebuild their church and community near Inez in Victoria County.

January 21, 1858—The Indianola Railroad Company is chartered to link with the San Antonio and Mexican Gulf line from Port Lavaca, but the South will be wracked by the Civil War and Reconstruction before the railroad is placed into operation.

January 31, 1858 —The first five miles of track of the San Antonio and Mexican Gulf Railroad are completed, from Port Lavaca to Clark's Station.

Spring 1858—Indianola gains its third newspaper, the *Indianola Courier and Commercial Bulletin,* with William T. Yancy at its helm, replacing the *Indianolian.*

July 1, 1858—Danish sea captain Peter Johnson gains a $4,950 per annum contract to carry the mail from Indianola to Corpus Christi, 150 miles and back, three times a week. Mail is taken by boat from Indianola to Saluria, where it is transferred to a mule-drawn stagecoach for the trip down Matagorda Island to Cedar Bayou. A ferry is used to transfer the coach to St. Joseph Island, and at Aransas the mail is transferred to a shallow draft boat for the final leg to Corpus Christi.

1859—As the population in West Texas swells, so does business at Indianola. During this year cotton exports increase 250 percent, barrels of goods moved across Indianola wharves rise 63 percent, and lumber imports are up 65 percent; wool is up 55 percent and hides, 43 percent. Business is booming!

The Courthouse is completed and a stout wooden fence is erected around the square with stiles for access rather than a gate that might be left open. The fence and stiles protect the Courthouse from loose livestock.

Lt. Col. Robert E. Lee returns to Washington, D.C., to administer the estate of his late father-in-law. While there he commands the company that captures abolitionist John Brown at Harper's Ferry.

Concerned that abolitionists might incite an armed insurrection by slaves, the Indianola Aldermen impose a 9:00 P.M. curfew on all blacks, slave or free, without written permission from their master, owner, or employer. Blacks are also restricted from playing cards or any gambling game within the city limits. Punishment is set at thirty-nine lashes or the payment of a fine.

Otto L. Schnaubert offers drawing lessons at Indianola. Sketching is a popular pastime, and he draws a large clientele.

February 21, 1859—George Hoeld obtains right to operate the ferries between Alligator Head (Port O'Connor) and Saluria.

February 22, 1859—Calhoun County Commissioners Court grants State Rep. James H. Duncan the right to operate a ferry over the Guadalupe River near Green Lake on the road from Indianola to Refugio. The site is also known as "White's Ferry."

Late July 1859—A new and brighter light is operational in the Matagorda Island Lighthouse. The light is a new third-order Fresnel lens ordered to replace the tower's old-fashioned reflectors. More plates are cast at the foundry in Baltimore and installed to make the tower twenty-four feet taller.

August 6, 1859—Samuel Addison White purchases the *Victoria Advocate,* which he will edit until 1867.

August 16, 1859—A jail cell constructed for the Courthouse has sat upon the beach for ten months where it was delivered. After suffering public ridicule, the Commissioners Court uses school funds to install the cell within the jail. A public toilet is installed in the Courthouse—another first for Indianola.

Also, funds are approved for the construction of a bridge over Stevens Bayou for easier access to the cemetery and the roadway to Green Lake.

September 1859—Two private schools are seeking students, the Indianola Male and Female School and the School for Boys and Girls.

Late 1859—Stones for a mill to be built in San Antonio by C. H. Guenther in San Antonio are imported from France and hauled to San Antonio from Indianola by ox teams, twelve oxen to a wagon.

1860s

1860 —Professor White, an accomplished musician and dance master, returns to Indianola from his summer vacation to reopen his school.

February 19, 1860—Lt. Col. Robert E. Lee returns to Indianola and assumes command of the 8th Military District at San Antonio.

March 15, 1860—Lee obtains an agreement from the Mexican government that it will halt forays by Juan Cortinas into Texas at Brownsville.

April 7, 1860—The directors of the Indianola Railroad Company meet to discuss how to raise funds to construct their line. They note that the Buffalo Bayou, Brazos and Colorado Railway Company succeeded in raising the money it needed by tapping investors in Massachusetts.

June 1860—Bilingual instruction (German and English) in Indianola schools ends when English is made the required language of instruction.

October 15, 1860—*William G. Hewes*, built for Charles Morgan's trade in the Gulf of Mexico, is launched at Wilmington, Delaware.

October 27, 1860—A packery owned by J. J. Harrison advertises "fresh green turtle meat and turtle soup" in the *Indianola Courier and Commercial Bulletin*. It is packed into two- and six-pound tins and "warranted to keep in any climate."

View of Indianola taken from the bark Texana, *September 1860. Drawn from nature by Helmuth Holtz from Ed. Lang Lithographical Establishment, Hamburg, Germany. Published by Helmuth Holtz, sole proprietor.*

— Courtesy Victoria College, Victoria, Texas

October 31, 1860—Johann Schwartz dies at his home at Powderhorn. The obituary published in the *Indianola Courier* on November 3, 1860, describes him as "the oldest inhabitant of Indianola, being the first settler on the present site of the city (Indianola) where he built the first house, which he occupied up until the hour of his death."

November 3, 1860—McBride's shipyard on Powderhorn Bayou has completed the steamer *A.B.* for the Texana trade and is overhauling the *Lizzie Lake* for the Guadalupe River. Southern Steamship Company is also adding steamers between New Orleans and Indianola.

Charles Morgan now has nine steamers operating between New Orleans and Matagorda Bay: *Charles Morgan, Mexico, Texas, Matagorda, Orizaba, Austin, Arizona, Atlantic,* and the *Suwannee.*

November 6, 1860—Abraham Lincoln is elected president of the United States by electoral vote but only 40 percent of the popular vote.

A mass meeting is organized at Indianola to resist "Black Republicanism." The nighttime parade includes twenty-eight "transparencies" painted on glass. Carried high on poles and backlit by candles and kerosene lamps, the transparencies are easily read by onlookers. One hundred and thirty-two residents sign a petition asking Gov. Sam Houston to secede Texas from the Union.

November 27, 1860—Maj. Gen. David Twiggs is brought out of retirement to resume command of the Department of Texas, a position held by Col. Robert E. Lee during the previous nine months. A month later Twiggs is asking his superiors what actions he should take if Texas votes to secede from the Union.

December 1860—Legendary cattleman Abel Head "Shanghai" Pierce meets his brother Jonathon, who has arrived at Indianola from Rhode Island aboard the *A.C. Leverette* after encountering, it is said, three hurricanes at sea. The two have not seen each other since childhood but together they will soon own one of the largest cattle operations in Texas.

Christmas 1860—Christmas Day feasts include turtle soup, roast goose, meat pies, broiled oysters, candied sweet potatoes, peas, asparagus, candied cherries, raisins, currants, dried figs, watermelon pickles, lemon meringue and pumpkin pies, plus cookie jars filled with lebkucken.

January 9, 1861—Two miles from Fort Sumter shots are fired across the bow of the *Star of the West.*

February 23, 1861—Texas votes to secede from the Union. Plans to raise money and construct the Indianola Railroad are dashed. Texas will formally declare its intention to join the Confederacy on March 2, 1861, Texas Independence Day.

February 25, 1861—An unhappy Col. Robert E. Lee departs from Indianola, ultimately to become Gen. Robert E. Lee of the Confederacy.

March 16, 1861—Gov. Sam Houston refuses to take the prescribed oath of allegiance to the Confederate States of America and begins packing to return to Huntsville. The lieutenant governor, Edward Clark, takes his place as governor.

March 26, 1861—CSA Col. Earl Van Dorn, a U.S. Army officer who has switched his allegiance to the Confederacy, is in Indianola to ask Maj. Edmund Kirby Smith and Lt. Thornton Washington to join the Confederate armies.

March 30, 1861—Hugh Walker Hawes, writing from Saluria, reports that there are five Federal transport vessels lying outside Pass Cavallo ready to receive Federal troops that are marching toward Indianola.

April 17, 1861—Federal troops still in Texas are en route to Indianola when Fort Sumter falls under bombardment by South Carolina guns. Concealed by darkness, Confederate troops from the *General Rusk* under the command of Col. Earl Van Dorn are able to board the *Star of the West* while it is anchored in Pass Cavallo.

The crew of the federal ship is overcome and the Confederates sail it away to Galveston Bay without alarming the crew of a nearby federal gunboat, the *Mohawk*, assigned to protect the *Star of the West.*

April 23-24, 1861—Volunteers flock to Victoria to form the Home Guard.

April 25, 1861—C. C. Sibley, major, Third Infantry, commanding, is forced to surrender to Colonel Van Dorn at Saluria because his men are blocked from escape by four Confederate steamers bearing more than 1,200 men. The captured Federals are allowed to sail to New York.

May 1861—Capt. Daniel Shea is directed to take a position at Pass Cavallo and to enroll a company of 100 men for one-year term.

May 9, 1861—On the El Paso road at San Lucas Springs between Castroville and San Antonio, a Confederate force under the direction of Colonel Van Dorn meets and captures the last column of Federal troops trying to leave Texas.

May 25, 1861—Matagorda Bay is one of five western Gulf of Mexico bays named by the *New York Commercial-Advertiser* that must be secured to make a Southern blockade of the Confederacy successful.

May 28, 1861—The U.S. Congress halts mail service in all states that have seceded, but the Confederate Congress has already established a Post Office Department which on June 1, 1861, will take over the routes formerly held by the federal government.

May 30, 1861—Indianola residents pledge $463 for the purchase of a cannon to defend Matagorda Island.

June 27, 1861—Indianola Company A Home Guard (Infantry) is organized and under the command of Capt. D. E. Crosand. It is the first group organized following the November 2, 1860, mass meeting at Indianola.

June 29, 1861—Indianola Company B Home Guard (Infantry) is organized under the command of Capt. Leon Rouff. An Indianola Artillery Company is also organized under the command of Capt. George Thielepape.

July 13, 1861—Calhoun County Commissioners Court appropriates $1,500 to purchase ammunition for the defense of the county.

September 27, 1861—Lavaca Guards under the command of Capt. Alexander Hamilton Phillips, Jr., are mustered into the Confederate Army and designated as Company A of the Sixth Texas Infantry Regiment.

December 7, 1861—A war sloop in Pass Cavallo opens fire on Fort Washington on Matagorda Island. Under Shea's direction the fort's twenty-four pounders respond, striking the sloop two or three times. The sloop withdraws from the pass.

Mid-December 1861—Shea's superiors agree that the batteries on Matagorda Island should be relocated from Fort Washington to a position opposite Pelican Island and Bird Island at the mouth of the pass. In addition, four companies of men are ordered to Saluria to protect the ferry across the main bayou. The new position is known as Camp Esperanza and then Fort Esperanza. Its earthen walls are built, in part, by slave labor.

1862—Ann Thomas of Port Lavaca, a "true Southern Rebel," nonetheless deplores the conduct of the Sixth Texas Infantry stationed at Port Lavaca. She writes that no house is safe from civilian or military personnel. Porches and roofs are torn down for use as firewood, and indigent women sometimes obtain the meal rations due to them only by threatening the public miller with pistols.

The Lavaca Guard raised by Capt. A. H. Phillips is insubordinate, cutting down the tent of Major Shea in one incident. Thomas adds that Phillips needs six men as a bodyguard at all times to keep his own men from killing him.

February 2, 1862—Maj. C. G. Forshey, major of artillery and engineer of coastal defense of the Confederate Army of Texas, observes that Pass Cavallo is secure but that the fort is vulnerable to an attack by land.

Most of the island's residents, like those of other Texas barrier islands, move to the mainland, anticipating an attack by the Federal gunboats that are patrolling the coastline. Few will ever return.

March 23, 1862—Gohmert's Theater at Yorktown, long popular with teamsters operating between Indianola and San Antonio, is blown down by a tornado.

March 27, 1862—More volunteers from Calhoun and Victoria counties are mustered into Confederate service to form Company H of the Sixth Texas Infantry Regiment under the command of George P. Finlay.

May 21, 1862—Calhoun County Commissioners Court orders the printing and issuance of currency, printed in denominations of twenty-five cents, fifty cents, $1, $2, and $3. When presented to the county treasurer the notes are redeemable in Confederate money. The commissioners also vote to move the county's archives to Victoria for safekeeping.

May 31, 1862—Confederates contract with John Graham at $4,750 per annum to provide mail service between Indianola and Corpus Christi via Saluria and Aransas.

July 1, 1862—Major Forshey prepares a map showing the location of old Fort Washington, the Pass Cavallo Lighthouse, the redoubts below Fort Esperanza, Saluria, and the road from Saluria to Indianola.

October 4, 1862—Galveston Bay falls to a naval attack by the Union.

October 26, 1862—The Federal fleet moves into Matagorda Bay to a position opposite Indianola. Under a flag of truce Capt. William B. Renshaw meets with a delegation representing Indianola's citizens. They refuse to supply the Federal troops with the provisions and beef the Federal troops demand. Indianola is given ninety minutes to evacuate women, children, and ill residents. Two Confederates are killed during the brief exchange of fire. Indianola is captured and looted.

October 31, 1862—Shea, accompanied by four Port Lavaca residents, meets with Captain Renshaw under a flag of truce and refuses to surrender. Again ninety minutes are allowed for evacuation before Federal troops open fire.

November 1, 1862—Three Yankee gunboats enter Pass Cav-

Author in 1863 dress at Indianola Courthouse Stone placed by County Commissioner Frank Wedig at Indianola during the 1960s. The stone marks the nearest point on land to the ruins of the Indianola Court-house, which now lie underwater about 100 yards from the shoreline.
— Courtesy Louise Popplewell

allo. Capt. J. M. Reuss with his company of Confederate soldiers on Matagorda Island fire their cannon, "Long Tom," and retreat to Indianola.

November 2, 1862—Lavaca is bombarded by Renshaw's forces but refuses to surrender despite an epidemic of yellow fever that is raging at the time.

Late November 1862—Federal troops withdraw from Matagorda Bay. The U.S. gunboat *Kittatinny* is ordered to move into the bay but is unable to do so because her draft is too deep. Confederate troops are able to reoccupy Fort Esperanza and command the channel.

Christmas Day 1862—Confederate General John Bankhead Magruder orders that the railroad ties and bridges at Indianola and the lighthouses at Saluria and Pass Cavallo are to be destroyed to prevent their capture by Federal troops.

New Year's Day 1863—Confederates rout Federal troops from Galveston Island. Capt. William B. Renshaw, who has recently shown Indianola and (Port) Lavaca only meager mercy, is killed when explosives he has set to booby trap a ship explode before he is able to depart to safety. The offshore blockade by Federal forces continues.

January 15, 1863—Shea reports to Magruder that all bridges and ferries linking Saluria and Indianola have been destroyed or removed.

February 1863—Capt. E. C. Singer of Lavaca develops and proves the world's first torpedo (or submarine mine) on the shores of Lavaca Bay and is consigned by the CSA to produce them.

February 4, 1863—Confederates regain control of Indianola. During eight months of 1863 a Confederate company under the command of Captain George of Seguin, Colonel Hobby's Regiment, is stationed there.

September 6, 1863—Felix A. Bluecher, major of artillery and assistant engineer, CSA, prepares a map of Pass Cavallo but the fort is shown as Fort Debray instead of Esperanza. A hospital is shown on the island side of the road from the fort to Saluria.

November 5, 1863—Indianola resident Fletcher S. Stockdale is elected lieutenant governor of Texas. Stockdale will become the state's interim head of state on June 11, 1865, when the Confederacy collapses and Gov. Pendleton Murrah flees to Mexico during the aftermath of Appomattox.

November 6, 1863—Brownsville is occupied by Federal troops, as is Port Isabel two days later, followed by Corpus Christi on November 16 and Aransas Pass the next day.

November 23, 1863—Federal troops reach Cedar Bayou which separates St. Joseph Island from Matagorda Island. After a brisk fight Federal troops construct flatboats and continue their advance northward.

November 27, 1863—Federal troops open fire on Fort Esperanza. During the night of November 29 the Confederate troops retreat to Indianola.

December 1863—Union troops proceed to Indianola, which they retake after a brief but spirited fight. One of their prizes is the flag made by the ladies of Indianola and presented to the Fort Esperanza troops.

December 31, 1863—A blue norther arrives on Matagorda Bay. Twenty men and boys of Captain Rugeley's Company of Confederates perish in Matagorda Bay.

January 4, 1864—The 22nd Iowa Volunteer Infantry and other Federal troops are ordered to Indianola.

January 27, 1864—Confederate troops mass at Caney Creek. The Federal forces halt their march to Houston and retreat from Matagorda Peninsula and gather at Indianola, leaving each side wary of attack by the other force.

February 13, 1864—Thirty-seven Union scouts "well-armed and mounted" inadvertently enter a 200-acre cattle corral at the Foester ranch, only to discover that a body of 75 Confederates is attempting to close the gates behind them. Their commander later wrote, "We had to cut our way through a body of 75 Rebels . . . with our sabers and pistols." Two of his men were unseated from their horses and roped by the Rebels before they could be rescued, he added.

February 22, 1864—Fourteen Union scouts ("not fully armed and grazing some horses who were lame") are captured eight miles from Indianola as they are rounding up some loose cattle for their camp at Indianola. Three of the Union scouts are wounded, and three horses are killed. The Confederates suffer losses too: seven men are killed, four men are wounded, and three horses are killed.

February 29, 1864— A series of rifle pits and "substantial forts" have been completed by the 22nd Iowa Regiment to defend "Old and New Indianola." During the next month the men will also dig a double row of zig-zag trenches across Matagorda Island.

Trenches and a series of redoubts dug across Matagorda Island by the 21st, 22nd, and 23rd Iowa Regiments can still be seen in this aerial view of Matagorda Island taken above the Gulf-side beach.

— Photo by author

March 13, 1864—Twenty-two men of the 69th Indiana Regiment drown when the ferry boat they are using to evacuate regimental goods from Indianola is swamped with water.

March 18, 1864—Confederate scouts discover that the Federal troops have abandoned Indianola, having retreated to Saluria. There the 16th Wisconsin is loaded onto five steamers and sixteen sailing vessels bound for Louisiana, but other units will remain on the island for another three months.

March 24, 1864—The 14th Rhode Island Regiment, a black regiment, threatens to mutiny on Matagorda Island. They are placed under guard by the 22nd Iowa Volunteer Infantry. The ringleaders are punished and the others are released.

April 6, 1864—Federal gunboats take several Confederate officers and men into custody at Indianola.

April 8, 1864—Federal forces suffer a decisive defeat at Mansfield, Louisiana, and they end their attempt to control Texas.

April 11, 1864—Voters approve moving the county seat back to Lavaca because some of the county officials at Indianola had taken the oath of allegiance to the United States during the occupation of Indianola by Federal troops.

April 9, 1865—Gen. Robert E. Lee surrenders at Appomattox.

June 19, 1865—Union Maj. Gen. Gordon Granger arrives in Galveston and proclaims the emancipation of slaves and the end of the Confederacy in Texas, thus freeing 175 slaves at Indianola valued at $62,400.

June 24, 1865—Federal blockade of Matagorda Bay is lifted, allowing commerce to resume. Soon after Federal troops under Maj. Gen. David S. Stanley, including 10,000 men of his Fourth Corps, arrive at Indianola for the military occupation of South Texas.

In New York City and Washington, D.C., Charles Morgan buys back ships taken from him by both sides of the recent conflict to rebuild his shipping empire.

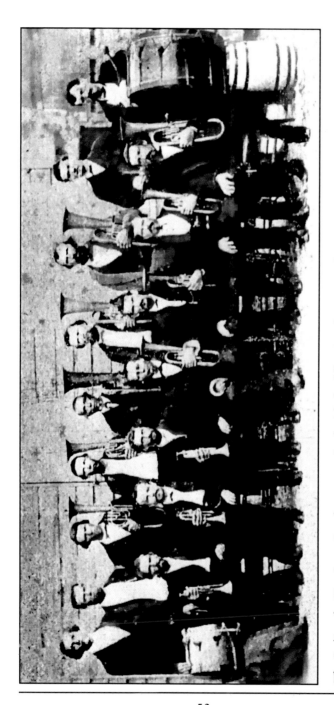

The Indianola City Brass Band was organized with the following charter members: Anton Bauer, Louis Budde, B. Evers, Louis Busch, C. H. French, John Freund, Fred Holzheuser, Philip Holzheuser, A. Mylius, H. Nitsche, G. Wassermann and C. Wolk. This photo shows three additional band members not named in the charter.

— Courtesy Institute of Texan Cultures, San Antonio

September 1865—The county seat is returned to Indianola along with the archives that had been stored at Victoria during the war.

December 10, 1865—Indianola City Brass Band is organized.

Prelude to the
Storm of 1875

1866—Indianola is struck by a severe storm but no lives are lost and no buildings are destroyed. A lumber vessel from Pensacola, Florida, is driven through the wharf by the wind and becomes grounded in front of the Casimir Hotel, where she will remain for months.

Indianola's fourth newspaper, the *Indianola Times,* is established under the leadership of S. A. Benton. The *Indianola Bulletin* (halted by paper shortages during the Civil War) resumes publication with C. A. Ogsbury again at its helm. Ogsbury will operate the *Bulletin* without interruption until the storm of 1875. He will then move inland to establish a newspaper at Cuero.

Robert Clark of Indianola and Charles Stillman of Brownsville resume operation of the meat-packing plant that was shut down during the war due to metal shortage.

Francis Stabler, who came to Indianola from Baltimore, also opens a canning factory; however, he uses carbonic acid gas in his process, producing a tastier product, according to *Indianola Bulletin* and the *Texas Almanac.*

Buck Taylor shoots a black sergeant who comes to arrest him for a minor infraction at a dance being held at the home of his uncle, Joe Tumlinson, near Yorktown. Soon afterward, Buck's brother, Hays, kills a black soldier in an Indianola saloon. They high tail it to Karnes County. In November 1867, Hays and Doboy Taylor will be involved in the shooting of two Yankee soldiers at Fort Mason. Hays and Doboy escape, but a $500 price is put on their heads.

February 1, 1866—Amnesty votes taken up January 8 are forwarded to Austin. The names of those who supported the Confederacy are stricken from these lists and they lose their right to vote.

August 15, 1866—San Antonio & Mexican Gulf Railroad between Port Lavaca and Victoria resumes daily service (except Sundays), having been rebuilt by the Federal government.

August 31, 1866—Trade through the port shows that Indianola is recovering. Imports include livestock, grocery items, whiskey, sugar, flour, nails, plows, coal oil, coffee, molasses, hay, corn, oats, coal, palmetto logs, lumber, shingles, laths, doors, and sash. Exports include cotton, wool, hides, pigs, lead, merchandise, tallow, pecans, pigs, copper, cotton seed, molasses, sheep skins, sumac nitre, corn, ice, mules, cattle, rope, goat skins, and beeswax.

October 19, 1866—State legislature renews charter for Indianola Railroad Company and allows the company until January 1, 1871, to complete the first fifteen miles of roadway.

1867—Carl Hilmar Guenther establishes an ice plant in San Antonio that will be operated for decades as Southern Ice Company before it is merged into Southern-Henke Ice Company.

January 4, 1867—Fourteen buildings burn because the Indianola Hook and Ladder Company has no pumper to pump water from the bay, only a short distance from the fire.

June 1867—Indianola and Galveston are revisited by yellow fever epidemic which soon becomes widespread throughout the state.

October 3, 1867—A storm making landfall at Galveston also causes widespread damage in Matagorda and Galveston bays.

1868—Max Krueger, a just-arrived sixteen-year-old German immigrant, devises a way to move the huge boilers brought to

A fire destroyed fourteen buildings at Indianola in January 1867 because the Indianola Hook and Ladder Company had no pumps to use water from the bay. Presidents: C. W. Short, Charley Burbank, Capt. Henry Sheppard. Members: Lehman, Linderman, Leonard, Andrew Dove, Dudley Schultz, Walter Seeligson, Willie Morrison, Tony Platz, Dan Sullivan, Charley Hogan, William Hogan, Jacob Ham, and Frank Coffin.

— Courtesy Institute of Texan Cultures, San Antonio

Indianola the four-mile distance from the wharf to the site where they are to be used for a meat-packing plant.

After making and losing one fortune, Krueger will amass a second one as founder and builder of the San Antonio Machine and Supply Company. By 1920 the company will have more than $1 million in capital, $645,000 in surplus, and plants in Corpus Christi, Waco, and San Antonio.

Henry Seeligson operates a meat packery at Indianola employing the Stabler process of curing meat by replacing the air with carbonic gas. Seeligson pays his Mexican labor $15 a month.

March 1868—William Sutton, a deputy sheriff representing the military police, leads a posse from Clinton in DeWitt County in pursuit of horse thieves. At Bastrop, Sutton shoots Charley Taylor. Taylor's companion, James Sharp, is then shot during the return trip. This marks the first incident between Sutton and the Taylors.

March 31, 1868—A city block in Indianola is purchased for the construction of a convent. At first only a small frame structure is built and it is used to house the St. Mary Institute and School.

Summer 1868—Quarantine station established at Indianola and at other Texas ports in an effort to control yellow fever epidemics.

November 28, 1868—E. A. Hensoldt files a map of Indianola at the Calhoun County Courthouse.

Christmas Eve, 1868—In a shootout at a Clinton saloon, Buck Taylor and Dick Chisholm are shot by William Sutton, representing Edmund J. Davis' State Police. The Taylors are outraged that they are unable to bring Sutton to trial.

1869—Samuel Addison White, Indianola's co-founder, dies during a trip to Indianola. The *Advocate's* editor-publisher, he had purchased the paper twelve years earlier. He is succeeded by James Boone, who would later be succeeded by Frank R. Pridham, sole proprietor of the *Advocate* until 1874.

February 25, 1869—Union occupation army orders all beef hides to be marked, and all captains of vessels on which cattle are shipped and all slaughterhouses to maintain register books to reduce hide and cattle rustling.

March 15, 1869—Strapped for cash, the Indianola Railroad Company sells two lots to Charles Morgan at the entrance to

View of the Indianola Cemetery, sometimes referred to as the "Lower Indianola Cemetery" to distinguish it from the Old Town Cemetery "On the Ridge." Markers at both cemeteries have been washed away by the storms of 1875, 1886, 1919, 1942, and Hurricane Carla in 1961. Many who died at Indianola were also buried in unmarked graves.
— Courtesy Henry Wolff, Jr.

the wharf. Morgan has set his sights on owning the Indianola Railroad Company as well as the San Antonio and Mexican Gulf Railway.

May 1869—Gas lights are installed to illuminate Indianola's business district, and Charles Morgan arrives from New York to inspect the port. He has quietly bought up majority interest in the Indianola Railroad. Concerned about railroads in the Midwest reaching Texas, Morgan urges San Antonio to construct a railroad that would connect with his railroad to Matagorda Bay. San Antonio rejects Morgan's offer to purchase $250,000 in stock.

July 10, 1869—World's first shipment of beef carcasses transported under refrigeration arrives at New Orleans aboard the Morgan steamship *Agnes*. Indianola was the ship's point of departure.

August 1869—A storm demolishes the sanctuary of the Episcopal Church of the Ascension, rips the roofs from several buildings, sinks boats, batters wharves and warehouses, breaks windows and topples chimneys, but there is no loss of life.

August 23, 1869—The military police lay an ambush that results in the killing of Hays Taylor. Under the direction of Jack Helm, military police are terrorizing all of the pasture lands between DeWitt County and Indianola on the coast under the guise of "catching rustlers."

September 23, 1869—Jack Helm publishes an account in the *Victoria Advocate* defending himself in his actions against the Taylor faction of the Sutton-Taylor feud.

1870—Indianola's population is 3,443, according to the federal census. Indianola also gains telegraph service. The Western Union telegraph line links Houston to Victoria, Indianola, Refugio, Corpus Christi, and Brownsville. In 1871 the line will be extended to include Mexico City.

April 1870—U.S. military authority is turned over to Governor Edmund J. Davis. One of his first acts is to push a police and militia bill through the state legislature. Thus begins the infamous state police organization placed under the direction of James Davidson to replace the military-sanctioned regulators. Davidson hires Jack Helm, who recruits Jim Cox, Joe Tumlinson, and Bill Sutton.

June 20, 1870—Indianola grants Morgan the right of way through its business district on payment of $1 and execution of a $50,000 bond by Morgan to ensure that at least sixty-five miles of track will be laid by May 1872.

August 26, 1870—State police under the direction of William Sutton arrest Henry and William Kelly, sons-in-law of Pitkin Taylor. A few miles from their home just south of Cuero they are shot to death while Mrs. Henry Kelly watches from a hiding place. State Sen. Bolivar Pridgen denounces the state police and Helm is dismissed. Sutton takes Helm's place.

1871—Construction of a fireproof vault in the Courthouse is authorized. With walls of solid bricks, sixteen inches in thickness and an interior height of seven feet six inches, the vault is expected to afford the county ample storage space for county records for several decades.

By 1871—Four baseball teams are organized: the Lone Star at Old Town, and the Stonewall Baseball Club, Excelsior and Crescent teams at Indianola proper. Also a streetcar system is established. The cars are drawn along a rail track by mules who walk between the rails.

April 3, 1871—State legislature authorizes the incorporation of the Indianola, San Antonio and El Paso Railroad. Its sponsors are businessmen who fear Charles Morgan and are seeking a way to bypass the Indianola Railroad that has just been linked to the San Antonio and Mexican Gulf Railway Company at Clark's Station. Sufficient capital cannot be raised, however, by the December 1871 deadline.

April 7, 1871—A new organ arrives for the Episcopal Church of the Ascension aboard the Morgan steamship *Morgan,* a gift from Charles Morgan.

April 12, 1871—Volunteer fire department at Indianola is authorized by the state legislature to incorporate as the Indianola Hook and Ladder Company.

April 20, 1871—Charles Morgan arrives from New York City accompanied by C. A. Weed, owner of the *New Orleans Picayune,* and Capt. Charles Fowler of Galveston. They and Morgan's other guests board the first train to ride the rails between Indianola and Clark's Station.

April 22, 1871—Morgan meets with the directors of the Indianola Railroad. Holding majority interest in it and the San Antonio and Mexican Gulf Railroad, Morgan merges them into a single corporation: the Gulf, West Texas and Pacific Railway Company.

May 16, 1871—A bell for the fire department arrives aboard the *W. G. Hewes* and is mounted on a tower at the truck house to sound the alarm when a fire is reported.

May 23, 1871—Railroad workers arrive from New Orleans to rebuild the roadbed between Clark's Station and Victoria and to extend the line westward to Cuero in DeWitt County, its intended destination.

June 1871—Rundell and Nolda, confectioners, fit up a magnificent saloon for lovers of ice cream. Also, iced soda waters are served.

The *Bolivar* inaugurates the first direct steamship service between Indianola and New York City.

June 3-9, 1871—Two storms batter the central Texas coast within days of each other. The first damages the *Alabama,* a steamship at Galveston, and causes the lower flats at Indianola to flood. The second storm floods the floors of the warehouses at Indianola and washes lumber from the lumberyards. Two or three small boats are run aground.

June 17, 1871—The Casino Society of Indianola enlarges its building to accommodate up to 400 people. Gas lights and a gymnasium are added as well. Public concerts of the Indianola City Brass Band and the Indianola *Saengerbund* are held there.

September 30, 1871—A storm floods the lower part of Indianola, causing widespread damage. Wind damage is minor but the highest water level ever is recorded since the town's earliest beginnings in 1844. At Lavaca, the jail is washed away and damage is reported to the railroad bridge at Chocolate Bayou and the railroad track above Indianola.

October 5, 1871—The Presbytery of Western Texas convenes at the Presbyterian Church at Indianola which can boast that it has the city's largest congregation. A bell for the church was shipped on the schooner *Franklin* in June, and the church's communion service was shipped aboard the *Carrie* in September.

October 18, 1871—Indianola Colored Benevolent Society is incorporated by Stephen Williams, Peter Thaupe, Jacob Harris, Philip Jones, Banister Prior, and Edward Peyton to assist needy blacks.

November 1871—Doboy Taylor gets into a dispute at Kerrville in regard to a cattle contract. During a struggle he is shot with his own gun.

December 6, 1871—A schooner, the *Thomas P. Ball*, built for the New York City to Indianola run, draws a crowd eager to inspect her as she ends her maiden voyage.

May 1872—U.S. Signal Service establishes a weather observation and reporting station at Indianola.

Summer 1872—Sympathizers of William Sutton lure Pitkin Taylor from his home near Cuero and he is shot. He dies of his wounds six months later. At the funeral, his son, Jim Taylor, vows to kill William Sutton. Soon after, Jim and cousins Bill Taylor and Alf Day shoot through the door of the Bank Saloon in an effort to end Sutton's life but Sutton is only wounded. They are jailed, but Wes Hardin and twelve other men cut them loose.

1873—During a visit to Germany, Max Krueger undertakes a six-month-long apprenticeship to learn photography. He invests his entire inheritance in a complete photography outfit and returns to Texas. In 1876 he will sell his equipment to Pius Fey, who will operate a studio at Cuero.

February 28, 1873—George Henry French is born at Indianola. He will later become publisher of the *Victoria Advocate* and at the time of his retirement will establish a record for retaining the *Advocate* for the longest period: forty-one years. He will publish, in 1936, *The Indianola Scrapbook* on the fiftieth anniversary of the 1886 storm.

March 4, 1873—First Gulf, West Texas and Pacific passenger train arrives in Cuero. Within two weeks nearly all of the business lots held by Cuero Land and Immigration Company are sold. Likewise, many of the residential lots in the Morgantown subdivision are sold.

April 1873—Over Governor Davis' veto, the state legislature abolishes the state police. Still, Jack Helm and a posse of fifty men show up at the home of Jim and Bill Taylor to take them into custody but are turned away by Jane Taylor, who insists that she has no knowledge of their whereabouts.

Wes Hardin, the Clements, and the Taylors are outraged and resolve to take matters in their own hands. In an ambush, Jim Cox is shot and his throat is cut from ear to ear. Also killed is a companion, John W. Cristman. Joe Tumlinson and three others narrowly escape.

May 17, 1873—At a blacksmith shop at Albuquerque, a small community in Gonzales County, Wes Hardin and Jim Taylor shoot Jack Helm to death and ride away. A month later they will make another attempt on the life of William Sutton but will only wound him.

August 11, 1873—Hardin and the Taylors besiege the Tumlinson home at Yorktown. A posse led by Deputy Sheriff D. J. Blair intervenes and the next day a formal truce is signed and recorded at Clinton Courthouse. The truce does not include the signature of William Sutton.

September 1, 1873—Matagorda Island Lighthouse becomes operational at its new and present-day site with the lens stationed ninety-six feet above sea level. The tower is painted solid black.

December 1873—The truce between the Taylors and Tumlinsons ends when Wiley Pridgen, a Taylor sympathizer, is killed at Thomaston.

February 17, 1874—Joseph G. Hardin (brother to John Wesley Hardin) and Aleck Barrickman visit Indianola to learn on what date and aboard what ship William Sutton and his pregnant wife, Laura, will depart from Texas.

March 11, 1874—William Sutton and Gabriel Slaughter are shot by cousins Bill and Jim Taylor as they are attempting to board the steamship *Clinton*. Laura screams hysterically as the two Taylors flee.

Jim rides to Gonzales County, where Wes Hardin is putting together a Kansas herd. Bill Taylor remains in DeWitt County and is nabbed by the town marshal, Rube Brown, while trying on a new pair of boots in a shop. Brown claims the $500 reward on Taylor's head.

June 20, 1874—Trail boss Doc Bockius and three boys, Kute Tuggle, Jim White and Scrap Taylor, are taken into custody near Hamilton and charged with rustling. A mob of thirty or more men storms the Clinton jail. Doc Bockius escapes, but the boys are hanged to avenge the death of William Sutton.

July 4, 1874 —A minor storm with gale-force winds causes minor damage to shipping interests at Indianola.

November 23, 1874 —Joe Tumlinson dies in bed, ending, at last, the Sutton-Taylor feud.

William "Bill" Sutton and Gabriel Slaughter are buried in Evergreen Cemetery at Victoria, Texas.

— Courtesy Henry Wolff, Jr.

Storm of 1875

1874 or 1875—*The Advocate* is purchased by Edward Linn and John A. McNeill. During his tenure, Linn will report on the lashing of Indianola by three storms: in 1875, 1880, and 1886.

September 1, 1875—First observation of the storm that will devastate Indianola is made by the crew of the *Tautallon Castle* southwest of the Cape Verde Islands off the coast of Africa. As the storm proceeds westward, ships that cross its path will lose their shiploads or their masts. Several will vanish entirely.

September 9, 1875—Storm reaches Barbados, causing vast destruction. It continues onto Haiti and Jamaica. More ships at sea disappear, among them the brigs *Serene* and *J. W. Spencer*.

September 13-14, 1875—Havoc is wrecked as eye of storm passes over Cuba. At Key West, vessels are driven ashore on the keys. Washington, D.C., sends warnings to Mobile, Alabama, but the storm veers westward targeting the Texas Gulf Coast.

September 14, 1875—Unaware of the storm in the Gulf, the Morgan steamship *Austin* departs Indianola with 388 head of cattle on board. Battered by the storm, the ship will limp into Sabine five days later with only twenty-five of the cattle still alive.

September 15, 1875—Gale force winds are accompanied by a falling barometer. Sgt. C. A. Smith begins hourly observations of what is clearly "more than a norther."

The streets of Indianola are filled with visitors from Victoria and DeWitt County who have come to watch the trial of Bill Taylor, who is charged with the murders of William Sutton and Gabriel Slaughter. Although the water level of the bay is reaching a new high, the Indianola residents are certain that the waters will recede.

September 16, 1875—At dawn the water has broken over the beach and is weakening the foundations of buildings. By midday the pounding waves are tearing apart the wharves. Residents and visitors alike use ropes to cross streets that are overflowing with fast-moving water. Panic spreads as it becomes apparent that they are trapped. The roads are impassable.

The passenger trains cannot run because the tracks are under water and the locomotives' water supply has become contaminated with salt water.

Hundreds crowd the Courthouse and the rising water forces them onto the second floor. Bill Taylor, George Blackburn, and Sam Ruschau are released from jail upon their pledge not to escape. They promptly steal horses and make their way across the flooded prairie.

Some lash cotton bales together to form rafts on which to escape from buildings that are about to collapse. Others float to higher ground by riding atop or clinging to the feather mattresses from their beds.

Claude Crosby floats his way to the depot by using a large wooden tub as a vessel. As he passes the Coutret home he waves to Alois Coutret, who was then a young boy. Twenty-one people are seeking shelter in the Coutret home. Later, another building floats against it, causing it to collapse. Alois is washed into the flood waters and lashed by debris. Hours later, swimming desperately to keep from being washed into the bay, he is pulled onto a raft by unknown hands only to discover that it is his brother Alex and another young friend, Charlie Walker. These three will be the only survivors from the Coutret home.

A large schooner is torn loose from her moorings and is

driven into the telegraph office, cutting off all contact with the outside world. By nightfall small dwellings and buildings will be swept away. A hide and wool warehouse behind the Signal Office collapses.

Mother Camillus and the nuns from the Sisters of Mercy of St. Patrick convent take refuge in the home of Robert Clark. The rising water forces them onto the second floor, but they are saved. The Catholic Church and convent are flattened as they watch.

September 17, 1875—During the brief period of calm when the eye of the storm passes over Indianola, Mrs. Robert Clark promises God that if she and her family are saved she will never return to Indianola in her lifetime. She will survive the storm and keep the promise.

The eye of the storm passes just after midnight. With the change in wind direction the water is driven back into the bay, causing even more damage to buildings that have already been weakened by the storm.

The quarantine station on Matagorda Peninsula is washed away. Dr. Fischer, the quarantine officer, his wife, Captains M. S. Mahon and Adolph Steinbach, and Martha Ellis survive by clinging for more than nine hours to the salt cedars that grow close to the hospital.

Survivors who venture out at dawn discover that three-quarters of all the town's buildings have been washed away and those that remain are in a state of ruin. The raft of debris extends twenty miles inland. Five bayous cut by the storm join Powderhorn Lake to the bay.

Bodies of victims are strewn along twenty miles of shore-line. The exact number who have died will never be known but is estimated to be at least 300. Most are buried where they are found.

Nearly all of those residing at Upper Saluria (near Mc-Henry Bayou) are drowned. Only one of the five Morgan steamship captains residing there survives: Capt. Sim Brown. Judge Hawes and other residents at Lower Saluria are saved by the higher elevation there.

The *Advocate* sends reporters by horseback and issues a

special edition flashing news of the destruction to the rest of the world. Communities throughout Texas respond by sending relief parties to aid the storm's victims.

The Morgan Steamship Line is particularly hard hit. The warehouse and wharves have been destroyed as well as the rolling stock on the track between Indianola and Chocolate Bayou.

C. A. Ogsbury, editor of the *Indianola Bulletin,* can find only some broken pieces of his printing press and scattered type where his newspaper office once stood. So ends publication of the *Indianola Bulletin.* He moves to Cuero.

Late September 1875—Indianola residents decide that their only hope for survival is to dredge a channel up Powderhorn Lake and rebuild on the lake's northern and most-inland shore. The ground is higher there and it is more than three miles from Powderhorn Bayou.

Several community leaders invite Charles Morgan's representatives, C. A. Whitney and A. C. Hutchinson of New Orleans, to visit Indianola and review their proposal. Whitney supports the proposal. Hutchinson is opposed. Morgan refuses to rebuild at a new location.

Aftermath—Many of Indianola's residents move to Port Lavaca, Victoria, Cuero, Texana, and San Antonio to start their lives anew. A few die-hard merchants rebuild their businesses at Indianola or establish branch operations at Victoria or Cuero. Indianola will never again reach the level of prosperity it once knew.

Late 1875—Marshal Rube Brown, who captured Bill Taylor in a Cuero boot shop, is gunned down "by unknown assailants."

November 19, 1875—Calhoun County Commissioners Court authorizes repairs to the Courthouse to include new steps, a door at one entrance, blinds on the cupola, shingles on the roof, and a new plank fence, fifteen feet high with a padlocked gate opening onto Main Street. A public privy is also built with two apartments, each with two seats.

December 27, 1875—Jim Taylor accompanied by Winchester

Smith and J. G. Hendrix ride into Clinton, some say to ask for a fair trial, others say to burn the Courthouse and all its records. A posse arrives, and a shootout ensues that leaves Jim Taylor and two of his friends dead.

Summer 1876—Aging, in ill health, and under the influence of his assistant, A. C. Hutchinson, Morgan abruptly halts all railroad service between Indianola to Cuero through Victoria, a ploy to force his business partners out of the company at Indianola's expense.

September 19, 1876—Several Suttons are implicated in the murder of Dr. Philip Brassel and his son George at their home near Yorktown. Eight men are charged with the crime. After twenty years of legal maneuvers, only Dave Augustine is convicted and then pardoned in 1896.

September 20, 1876—Morgan resumes rail service between Indianola and Cuero through Victoria. Tracks from Clark's Station to Port Lavaca damaged by the storm are removed, leaving Port Lavaca without rail service.

1878—Five Brahman cattle are unloaded at Indianola from a Dutch trading vessel. They are the first to be delivered to a Texas port and are quickly purchased by Capt. John N. Keeran and A. H. "Shanghai" Pierce.

May 8, 1878—Charles Morgan dies and Charles A. Whitney becomes president of Morgan's Louisiana and Texas Railroad and Steamship Company.

June 9, 1878—The *Victoria Advocate* reports that Bill Taylor, charged with the murder of William Sutton at Indianola in 1874, has been acquitted. Taylor is allowed to give bail in the sum of $5,000 in the murder of Gabriel Slaughter. The trial was heard in Texana before Judge William Buckhardt. Taylor is represented by four attorneys, Lackey and Stayton of Victoria, F. M. White of Jackson, and General Woodward of Indianola.

July 19, 1879—The case of Bill Taylor, charged with the murder of Gabe Slaughter at Indianola in 1874, is again before the court with the state asking for continuance. The request is denied, freeing Taylor unless a Calhoun County grand jury should indict him.

August 19-22, 1879—A storm that crosses Galveston causes only slight damage in the Matagorda Bay area.

January 17, 1880—The *Victoria Advocate* reports that writs have been issued for Bill Taylor and for another man named Middleton at Cuero for the rape of the young daughter of a "peaceable colored man." A third man, Frank Blair, was implicated but not charged. After that, it is said, Bill Taylor has left "this part of the country."

August 21, 1880—The *Advocate* reports that "On Wednesday of last week at 10:45 A.M., a cyclone struck this place." An unsigned letter describes the storm as having all the appearance of the 1875 storm except that the water did not break over the beach. Winds were recorded at 75 miles per hour at 2:30 A.M. on August 13 and there was more than seven inches of rain.

November 1882—Charles A. Whitney dies in New York of a massive stroke just as he is scheduled to depart for Europe. There he hoped to secure funding that would link Indianola with the West Coast by completing the rail line between Cuero and San Antonio.

January 12, 1883—Indianola has lost the race. A spike is driven that links the Galveston, Harrisburg and San Antonio Railway to the southern transcontinental rail line.

April 25, 1885—The *Victoria Advocate* reports that a three-day gale has caused unusually high tides at Indianola.

September 17-23, 1885—The *Victoria Advocate* reports that a storm originating east of Vera Cruz, Mexico, has skirted the Texas coast. The streets at Indianola are flooded and gullies are cut across the streets. Winds are reported at 45 miles per hour.

June 13-15, 1886—A tropical storm passes near Matagorda Bay but goes inland on the Louisiana coast at Lake Charles.

August 1886—Indianola attempts to rebuild as a resort but its population has dwindled to about 200 residents.

Shown are two ginger beer bottles found at Indianola. C. F. Vollers, owner of the Temperance Hall, advertised that he served "Lemon - ade, Ginger Beer with Ice, also a good Cigar and Oysters, Sardines or something else to keep the stomach in order."

— Photo by author

Storm of 1886

August 18, 1886—Indianola Signal Service observer Isaac A. Reed receives a telegram from Washington, D.C., warning that a West Indies hurricane has passed south of Key West into the Gulf of Mexico but is given no order to hoist a signal.

August 19, 1886—Isaac A. Reed receives signal to post a warning signal late on the night of August 19, but the storm is already well under way. Reed screws down the anemograph moments before he is persuaded to leave the building. Dr. H. Rosencranz and Reed reach the sidewalk but are caught by falling timbers; they drown.

A kerosene lamp left burning during Reed's hasty escape explodes and ignites a fire that spreads to the town's adjoining buildings. Destroyed in the inferno fanned by 102 mile-per-hour winds are A. Frank's warehouse, Lagus' grocery store, the Steinbach Market, and Villeneuve's liquor store.

The fire leaps to the west side of the street to take Dahme's Corner, Lagus' Hotel, Regan's Dry Goods Store, Lewis' Drug Store, the Anton Bauer home, and several other structures.

Young Frank Bauer and a friend, Cot Plummer, are on Matagorda Bay aboard the *Eclipse*, a forty-five-foot schooner, when the storm hits. Bauer survives by clinging to a plank with a black moccasin snake coiled up on the other end.

Anna Holzheuser, the five-year-old daughter of George Holzheuser (foreman for the Indianola Railroad), watches as a group of blacks seek shelter in a boxcar on the track near the railroad's maintenance shop, "the last structure beyond the bayou toward's Clark Station upon the Prairie." The force of the storm's wind pushes the boxcars carrying these refugees inland and to safety onto the higher ground of the prairie. The boxcar escape "at about 40 miles per hour" from the storm was also described after the storm by James Hatch in his memoirs.

August 20, 1886—Full force of the storm hits Indianola. The railroad track is washed away for two and a half miles outside of town. The storm overturns a train engine, two coaches, and a mail car. The depot and the roundhouse are left in ruins.

After the storm the only relic of Huck's lumberyard to be found is a safe. Runge's bank survives but is moved several feet. Dan Sullivan's and Runge's grocery stores are blown away.

The Presbyterian Church, the Methodist Church, "two

H. Runge & Company bank, store and warehouse with only the bank left standing. Huddled in the bank during the storm were Dr. David Lewis' wife, Amelia, and their four children; Anton and Katie Bauer with their six children; Louis Budde; Gus Wasserman; "and several colored people who had hairbredth escapes."   All survived. Dr. David Lewis was drowned trying to reach safety.
— Courtesy Victoria College, Victoria, Texas

Damage from the 1886 Storm—Shown is the area on East Main Street damaged by the fire that started when a kerosene lamp was overturned at the U.S. Signal Office. Shown also is the Anton Lagus cottage which sheltered eleven people who survived the storm.

— Courtesy Victoria College, Victoria, Texas

Damage from the 1886 Storm—Shown is the George French home with the upper story blown over the kitchen. Not a board was found of the lower story. At extreme left is the William Polk Milby residence.

— Courtesy Victoria College, Victoria, Texas

colored churches," and the high school are destroyed. The Catholic Church survives. A statue, *Mary, Star of the Sea,* had been placed in it for protection following the 1875 storm.

Home of Emil Reiffert receives only a little damage. Later the Reiffert home and about twenty others will be dismantled and rebuilt in Victoria and Cuero. At least two homes will be moved to Port Lavaca.

At Pass Cavallo island residents seek shelter in the lighthouse. The water rises four feet within the tower. Rocked by the storm's wind, one of the tower's flash panels and the first prism ring of the lens fall and shatter.

September 15-24, 1886—Only a month after the Great Indianola Storm, another storm is spawned that comes ashore just west of Corpus Christi and passes west of Victoria on September 23 and then northeastward out of Texas. Twenty miles of the New York, Texas and Mexican Railway track are damaged between Edna and Wharton, stopping trains for two days.

October 1, 1886—An excursion train is run to Indianola for those who wish to inspect the damage there. All seats are sold.

October 12, 1886—A hurricane develops south of Cuba then comes ashore at Sabine Pass. The death toll is estimated at 150.

November 2, 1886—Calhoun County residents vote to move the county seat back to Lavaca, which then takes on the name of Port Lavaca.

April 1887—A fire burns all of the buildings at Indianola not destroyed by the storm of 1886. The Gulf, West Texas and Pacific Railway Company gains permission to abandon fifteen miles of track between Indianola and Clark's Station.

May 7, 1887—The *Advocate* reports that government authorities have decided to abandon Indianola as a site for the post office.

June 18, 1887—A free excursion train is run from Cuero and Victoria to Indianola, its final run. The rails are relaid between Clark's Station and Port Lavaca by George Holzheuser, construction foreman for Southern Pacific, to restore service between Port Lavaca, Victoria, and Cuero.

October 4, 1887—John Mahon, Indianola postmaster, closes the door to the post office for all time. Indianola is officially declared to be dead. It has been forty-one years, twenty-one days since the community's first post office was opened at Indian Point by John W. Pope.

— Photo by author

Saluria and
Matagorda Island

Saluria and the Island
1837–1887

If the success of a community is measured by its churches, schools, trade and commerce, Saluria's heyday on Matagorda Island was between 1839 and the outbreak of the Civil War.

But to understand the settlement of Matagorda Island we must begin with Stephen F. Austin's first trip to Texas in 1821, when he was accompanied by a young Irish physician, James Hewetson. By some accounts it was in New Orleans, before their departure, that Hewetson introduced Austin to another young immigrant, James Power, who was then engaged in the mercantile business. Power, said to be a kinsman of Hewetson, was enthralled with the idea of establishing a colony in Texas, but he did not accompany the two men on their first trip to Texas.

At San Antonio Hewetson continued on to Mexico and established himself in the manufacturing and mercantile business at Saltillo and Monclova, eventually becoming an influential figure in Coahulitexan governmental circles. Later Power and Hewetson became partners and obtained a concession from the Mexican government to settle 400 families along the Texas Gulf Coast between the Nueces and Guadalupe rivers.

In addition to these headrights they purchased additional lands directly from the Coahulitexan government that included the shores of Copano and Aransas bays, the whole of Live Oak, Lookout and St. Charles peninsulas, and nearly all of Mustang, Harbor, Hog, St. Joseph, and Matagorda islands.

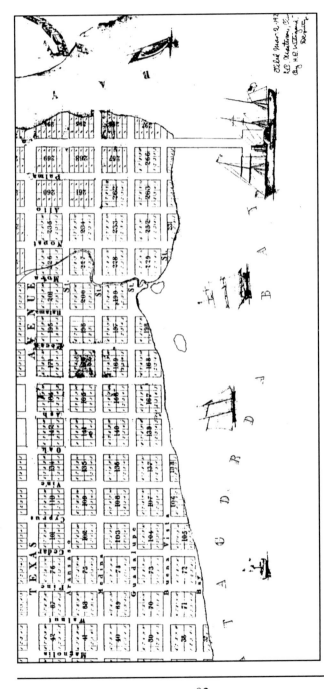

Detail from a map of Saluria drawn by E. Linn. Note terminus of Mexico, Gulf and San Antonio River Railroad at McHenry Bayou. Today a line of telephone poles installed by the U.S. Army during World War II can be seen along what would have been Texas Avenue. The map was discovered recently in a U.S. District Court file in Victoria, Texas.

Hewetson, involved with his business and land interests in Mexico, delegated the troubles and decisions arising from their Texas colonization efforts to James Power.

Joseph F. Smith began filing title to Power's lands in 1839, challenging Power's purchase of the land with only the consent of the Coahulitexan government.

An act of the U.S. Congress on January 28, 1839, required the secretary of the treasury to lay off 640 acres at the east end of Matagorda Island into a townsite to be named the City of Calhoun, which was to include a location for a customs house. Little is known about Calhoun, but the townsite apparently did not meet with much success because by February 2, 1844, the proposed location of the customs house was moved from Calhoun to Port Caballo on Matagorda Peninsula.

When the U.S. government abandoned the Calhoun townsite, Power projected a townsite of his own, Saluria, abutting McHenry Bayou.

On March 17, 1847 (St. Patrick's Day), Power made a contract with Gen. Alexander Somervell, John Washington Rose, and J. W. Dennison by which title to the 640-acre Saluria townsite was deeded to Somervell as agent and trustee. The new proprietors obligated themselves to subdivide the section into town lots and streets and were to reconvey to Power one-fourth of them. The remaining lots were to be sold and profits divided equally among the four parties. All unsold lots belonging to the three-quarter shares were to be divided four ways.

In addition to the Saluria townsite, Power also gave deeds at various times to tracts adjoining the townsite. In 1856 the legislature enacted a law confirming title of these tracts to the purchasers.

Other names mentioned in deed records during the 1840s include Edward Belden of Edward & Belden, L. K. Bryan, Rezin Byrne, Hugh W. Hawes, Corilla Hawes, Edward Linn, Joseph Lovitt, William Nichols, George Parr of Parr & Belden, Elizabeth M. Perry, Theodore Ryon, J. L. Shanks, Mary J. Smith, John Speer, Juliet Stanton, John B. Tucker, J. O. Wheeler, and David Williams.

Meanwhile Joseph Smith was still challenging Power's and Hewetson's claims to lands they had purchased from the Coahulitexan government without the permission of Mexico's supreme executive.

A review of the island's census records, mortality schedules, agricultural reports, and deed records reveals that Saluria was once a thriving community, with schools, churches and businesses, and that the island's stock raisers preferred sheep over cattle. But life was never easy on Matagorda Island.

1850 Census

When the first census was taken in 1850, the island's free population included sixty-eight males and fifty-two females. Of these, twenty-three were born in a "foreign" country and ninety-seven were born in the U.S. The value of the island's real estate was given as $51,400.

Countries of origin included England, Ireland, Wales, Canada, Denmark, Germany, and Mexico. States listed as origin (other than Texas) included Alabama, Connecticut, Illinois, Indiana, Kentucky, Louisiana, Maine, Maryland, Massachusetts, Mississippi, and New York.

The 1850 census also states that the slave population included twenty-two males and twenty-two females but their names are not given. Those who owned slaves were James P. McRainy, Thomas M. Duke, W. Varnell, James Cummings, John G. Hoffman, William Nichols, John W. Rose, Claiborn Hill, and S. S. Givens.

The island's population was young. The oldest resident on the island was Ann Horrell, sixty-two, of Maryland, residing in the home of Alexander Somervell, collector of customs. Forty-six of the island's residents were children aged twelve or younger; another dozen were in their teens.

Life on the island was not easy. The only source of fresh water was from rain water caught in cisterns. According to the 1850 Mortality Census, fourteen Calhoun County residents had died during the previous year. Causes of death included consumption (tuberculosis), cholera, fever, pneumonia, or inflammation.

Professionals on the island included John R. Baker of Tennessee, grocer; Thomas Brown of Maine and John Whelby, both Methodist clergy; S. S. Givens, merchant; Dr. Jacob Hall, physician; Dr. James P. McRainy of Tennessee, physician; John O. Oliver of Massachusetts, merchant; John Washington Rose of Mississippi, lawyer; and Alexander Somervell, collector of customs.

In his epic-length history of Refugio County, Hobart Huson stated that the populations of Matagorda and St. Joseph's islands were largely interchangeable. Many of the early settlers were captains of seagoing vessels and a number of them had served in the Texian Navy, Huson wrote. It is not surprising, then, that many of the island's residents revealed their connection to the sea by listing their occupation as sailor, shipwright, ship carpenter, or boatman.

Among these were William Cobbon, ship carpenter; James Cummings, sailor (and later to become the first keeper of the Matagorda Island Light), Thomas Harrison, sailor; William Hill, sailor; R. J. Holbin (or Halbin), shipwright; William Nichol, sailor; John B. Tucker, sailor, and W. J. Ward, boatman.

Other workmen on the island included Isaiah Lewis, carpenter; Samuel McBride, carpenter; Hans Schmidt, blacksmith; William Stukes, cabinet maker; and James Whillip, carpenter.

The Matagorda Island Lighthouse was built in 1852 overlooking Pass Cavallo, nearly two miles from its present-day location. Murray and Hazelhurst of Baltimore were awarded the contract to construct the Bolivar Point and Matagorda Island lighthouses.

The lighthouse was constructed of cast iron plates bolted together. The plates were cast in Baltimore and arrived aboard the brig *Russell* with Capt. E. K. Cooper at its helm in May of 1852. The Bolivar Lighthouse was assembled first and then the lighthouse on Matagorda Island.

The Matagorda Island Lighthouse was the first to be lit on the Texas Gulf Coast. Performing the honors was James E. Cummings, the light's first keeper, on New Year's Eve, 1852.

— Photo by author

The original paint scheme had horizontal red, white, and black bands. The tower was first lit on New Year's Eve of 1852 by James Cummings, the first keeper of the light, amid cheers from the crowds that had gathered for the event accompanied by whistle blasts from steamers in the bay.

In 1856 the residents of Saluria were probably among the hundreds that flocked to Indianola to see the U.S. Army camels unloaded from the *Fashion* after being transferred from the U.S. Navy store ship *Supply.*

Despite the island's harsh climate there were those who attempted to introduce agriculture on the island, including Jonathan Dunohoe, Thomas M. Duke, Daniel England, William Huntsman, George Morgan, Philip Rahal, Jacob Robertson, C. W. Vandeveer, and William Varnell.

1860 Census

By 1860 the free population on Matagorda Island had grown to 200 residents, including the island's lighthouse keeper, Thomas Hanson, seventy-three, born in South Carolina; and schoolteacher Joseph Bickford, twenty-seven, of New Hampshire.

Listed as a lawyer is Hugh Walker Hawes, whose descendants would be forced at the outbreak of World War II to sell the surface rights of their land so that an airbase and bombing range could be established on the island.

In addition to Hawes, two other attorneys are listed: R. A. Davage, born in Kentucky, and S. T. Seawell, forty-three, born in Virginia. The island's resident physician was J. W. McCreary, born in Tennessee.

Although there are no stock raisers listed in the 1850 census, ten claim that occupation in 1860, including Lauretta Brown, fifty, born in Maine.

Also, according to the 1860 census the island was home to forty-nine slaves, twenty-five male and twenty-four female. Thirty-one are described as black and twenty-two as mulatto.

H. W. Hawes was the largest slave owner with twenty-seven residing in three slave houses. Dr. McCreary had nine slaves in one house. The census notes that slaves formerly held by N. A. Milton, H. W. Sessions, William Nichols, James Mainland, and L. Dubois have been manumitted or set free.

Among residents named in the 1860 census that were not named a decade earlier were Osmer Bailey, James Bethel, William Ellin, Robert Gamble, P. H. James, James Mainland, Robert Rhodes, Joseph Smith, W. W. Warren, and Robert Wilkerson, who all listed their occupation as sailor, carpenter, or ship carpenter.

S. L. Townsend listed his occupation as lumber merchant. Other merchants included N. A. Milton, H. W. Sessions, and T. C. Taylor.

Mystery surrounds five homes occupied by thirty-six men, ranging in age from twenty-two to forty, without families. Two from Germany, one from Scotland, one from England and the other thirty-two from Ireland. Their occupation is listed as laborer but there is no clue as to what kind of labor they were performing. Perhaps they were railroad workers employed to build the bed for the Indianola Railroad. But if that were so, why not live at Indianola rather than on the island? Another possibility is that they were employed by the island's stock raisers, who were primarily raising sheep. Were these men eager immigrants working to pay for their passage to Texas?

Life on the island in 1860 appears to be no easier than in 1850. According to the mortality schedule for the previous year, G. N. Parks, thirty-five, a trader from South Carolina, committed suicide by cutting his throat with a razor and James Logan, twenty-eight, a lawyer born in Virginia, died of "intemperance."

George Hoeld, fifty-one, who had taken over operating the ferry across Saluria and McHenry Bayous from H. W. Hawes, died of injuries he suffered in a fight. John F. Smith, forty-eight, a tavern keeper born in New York, died of yellow fever, which also claimed the lives of his wife and three children, all during the month of November.

Other causes of death listed included meningitis, consumption (tuberculosis), convulsions, and "spasms."

Just before the outbreak of the Civil War the court ruled

in favor of Joseph Smith in his claims on lands formerly held by Power and Hewetson, but the titles on Matagorda Island were protected by the actions taken by the Texas Legislature in 1856.

1870 Census

The thirty-six laborers that are a mystery in the 1860 census cannot be found in the 1870 census. By then, however, the Civil War had taken its toll on Matagorda Island. The population dropped from 248 in 1860 to 156 in 1870.

Thomas Harrison, eighteen, a native Texan, is named as the Saluria lightkeeper. Almond Reed, sixty-nine, born in New York, is named as assistant lightkeeper.

Census records no longer record "free" and "slave" populations. They are now defined as white or black. The island's white population has declined to seventy-seven males and sixty-nine females. Only ten blacks are recorded on the island in 1870. All are employed as domestic servants. Some of these have apparently assumed the surnames of their former owners. Listed in the Hawes household are Nathaniel Hawes, twenty, Elizabeth Hawes, and Thomas Lacy. Antois Munson, nineteen, Kitty Smith, twenty-three, and Minnie Henderson, fourteen, are listed in the Horton household. Manual McNeal, forty-two, and Elizabeth McNeal, forty-two, are in the James Mainland household.

Only two deaths are recorded for the previous year: Jane Wilkinson, fifty-four, born in England, who died of typhoid fever, and a five-month-old girl, Emily Bunker. The census does not record whether Emily is the daughter of Theodius Bunker, twenty-seven, a cattle driver born in New York and Mary, twenty-four, born in Louisiana, or Nora Bunker, eighteen, a schoolteacher residing on the island.

According to the agricultural report, H. W. Hawes had four horses and 75 sheep valued at $325. He also reported 200 pounds of wool and that he sold or slaughtered animals valued at $36.

Almond Reed, the Saluria lightkeeper, had one horse, two work oxen, 30 other cattle, 100 sheep, 25 swine, and 250 pounds of wool valued at $525.

John Little had six acres of improved land valued at $600, 170 horses, 500 other cattle, 1,500 sheep, all valued at $6,540. For production he reported 90 bushels of Indian corn, 3,600 pounds of wool, 15 bushels sweet potatoes, 70 gallons of molasses and livestock sold or slaughtered, all valued at $382.

In May 1872 the U.S. Signal Service established a weather observation and reporting station at Indianola.

And on September 1, 1873, the Matagorda Lighthouse became operational at its new and present-day site.

1880 Census

After the devastating storm of 1875, the island's population continued to decline. Only forty males and thirty-two females are listed in the 1880 census. Of these, six are black, including Bettie Mead (who will die in the 1886 storm with two children not yet born when the 1880 census was taken).

The island's remaining residents represent only sixteen households. Surnames listed include Bloodworth, Cherry, Court, Farwell, Franks, Glenn, Hawes, Hays, Lake, Little, Madden, McMillan, Reynolds, and Wilkinson.

For many the devastation of the Civil War and the 1875 storm has been overwhelming. Residents have abandoned their dreams and moved to more hospitable lands on the mainland. Unpaid taxes on abandoned lands revert their title back to the state of Texas.

And the storm of 1886 is yet to come. . . .

A History of the Matagorda Island Lighthouse

Scheduled passenger traffic in Matagorda Bay began in 1840 when the shipping firm of Ferguson and Harrel began weekly passenger and freight service between Texana and DeCrow's Point on Matagorda Peninsula with a small paddle-wheel steamer known as the *Swan*. By 1844 Henri Castro and his leading competitor, Prince Carl of Solms-Braunfels, were both unloading their would-be colonists.

Recognizing the need for navigational aids, the Republic of Texas set aside $1,500 on February 3, 1845, for the purchase of land at Port Calhoun on Matagorda Island for a tower and "the necessary apparatus of a light."

The Republic of Texas became the twenty-eighth state of the United States of America on February 19, 1846. The following year, on March 3, the U.S. Congress allocated $30,000 for the construction of two lighthouses to be built on the Texas coast, one at Galveston (Bolivar Point) and the other at Pass Cavallo.

On November 22, 1847, the federal government purchased 2.5 acres of land on Matagorda Island from Thomas Jefferson Chambers overlooking Pass Cavallo at Calhoun for $250. Another five acres was purchased from Chambers on December 9, 1848, for $500.

Meanwhile a stagecoach line was established from Port Lavaca to New Braunfels via Victoria, Cuero, and Gonzales in November 1847, and two months later the brig *Matagorda* inaugurated service between Indianola and New York City. In that same month a weekly stagecoach service was established by J. B. Brown between Indianola and Victoria, timed to meet the departures and arrivals of the steamship *Yacht*. Owned by the New Orleans shipping firm of Harris and Morgan, the *Yacht* was providing weekly service between Galveston and Port Lavaca with a stop at Indian Point.

Clearly, traffic into Matagorda Bay was increasing by leaps and bounds as was the demand for the lighthouses that had been promised by the federal government. But construction of the lighthouses was delayed because the federal government could not proceed until the Texas Legislature gave the federal government full legal jurisdiction over the sites they had purchased.

By this time steamships sailing from Boston, New York, Philadelphia, Pensacola, Mobile, and lesser Gulf of Mexico ports were crowding the four wharves at Indian Point.

The bill granting the federal government full legal jurisdiction over the site purchased for the lighthouse on Matagorda Island was approved by the Texas Legislature on December 19, 1849, but the bill would languish on the governor's desk for nearly two years, unsigned.

During all this time there were no lights on the Texas Gulf Coast, leaving sea captains at the mercy of uncertain maps and the shifting shoals to be found in the passes.

In 1851 the *Palmetto* ran aground at Pass Cavallo. No lives were lost but the cargo and passenger baggage were ruined. Charles Morgan ended all stops by his ships at Saluria on Matagorda Island.

Finally, the governor signed the bill giving the federal government legal jurisdiction over the lighthouse sites. In October 1851, a contract was signed with Murray and Hazelhurst of Baltimore to fabricate and erect the two lighthouses for a total of $23,400. The reflector-type lighting apparatus was provided by Henry N. Cooper and Company of Boston.

Six lives were lost when the steamship *Independence* capsized in Pass Cavallo during a storm on March 26, 1852.

In May 1852 the brig *Russell* with Capt. E. K. Cooper arrived with the prefabricated plates for the cast-iron lighthouse to be placed on Matagorda Island after having first discharged the plates for the Bolivar Point Lighthouse. On June 20 it was reported that all the materials were on the island except for the brick. The cast-iron plates on Matagorda Island were bolted together to create a fifty-four-foot-tall iron tower lined with bricks for extra strength.

The various delays caused the Murray and Hazelhurst crew to work on the lights during the dreaded yellow fever season of late summer and early fall. The tower was completed by September 29, 1852, but installation of the reflector-type lens was not complete until Christmas Day.

On December 31, 1852, hundreds gathered on the waterfront at Indianola. When the first flash was seen, the crowd erupted into cheers. Some fired their firearms into the air. Steamers in the bay blew their whistles.

At last the seaports of Saluria and Indianola had a light tower! Performing the honor was Capt. James Cummings, the first lightkeeper.

Although the Point Bolivar tower on Galveston Bay was constructed first, the Matagorda Island Light was the first on the Texas coast to be lit. The Bolivar Point tower was not lit until twenty days later.

But still the Matagorda Island light had its problems. New ventilators were cut during the summer of 1853 to provide more airflow around the lamps.

The tower was not painted until the spring of 1854, when white, red and black horizontal bands were added so that it would be more easily seen during daylight hours.

A few months later the tower suffered its first substantial storm. The lantern, reflectors, and the keeper's dwelling all required repairs. Wire netting was added to keep birds from flying into the light at night.

By then a more serious problem was becoming apparent. The strong currents of Pass Cavallo were rapidly eroding the bank upon which the tower and keeper's house were built. The keeper's house was moved, but no action was taken to protect the tower.

It was also clear that the tower wasn't tall enough or

bright enough to be seen by the sea captains that needed her most. In July 1857 Murray and Hazelhurst cast more plates at the Baltimore foundry so that the tower's height could be increased by another twenty-four feet.

A new third-order Fresnel lens was ordered to replace the old-fashioned reflectors. The new light from the taller tower was operational by late July 1859.

Before the outbreak of the Civil War a swash point light was installed at the entrance to Pass Cavallo near the tip of Matagorda Peninsula. This was a wooden structure built over the water and attached to pilings that were screwed, not pounded, into the bay bottom.

On January 9, 1861, two shots were fired across the bow of the *Star of the West.* On February 23, Texas voted to secede from the Union and joined the Confederacy on March 5. Six weeks later, on April 17, the *Star of the West* was captured by the Confederates in the Gulf within sight of the Matagorda Island Lighthouse.

Maj. C. C. Sibley, Third Infantry, commanding, was forced to surrender to CSA Colonel Van Dorn at Saluria because his men were blocked from escape by four steamers bearing more than 1,200 men. The captured Federals were allowed to sail for New York.

According to the *New York Commercial-Advertiser* on May 25, 1861, Matagorda Bay was one of five Gulf of Mexico bays that needed to be secured by the Union if a blockade of Southern ports was to succeed. CSA Captain Daniel Shea was directed to take a position at Pass Cavallo. He was also authorized to enroll a company of 100 men for a term of twelve months.

A war sloop in Pass Cavallo opened fire on Fort Washington on Matagorda Island on December 7, 1861. Under Shea's direction the fort's twenty-four-pounders responded, striking the sloop two or three times. A week later Shea's superiors agreed that the batteries on Matagorda Island should be relocated opposite Pelican Island and Bird Island at the mouth of the pass. Also four companies of men were ordered to Saluria to protect the ferry across the main bayou.

The new position was known as Camp Esperanza and then Fort Esperanza. Its earthen walls were built, in part, by slave labor. Well before the end of 1861 (the exact date is not known) the Matagorda Island light was extinguished so that it would not aid Federal gunboats that were enforcing a block-ade of Southern ports.

CSA Major C. G. Forshey, major of artillery and engineer of coastal defense of the Confederate Army of Texas, ob-served on February 2, 1862, that Pass Cavallo was secure but that the fort was vulnerable to an attack by land. Most of the island's residents, like those of other Texas barrier islands, were ordered to move to the mainland in anticipation that Federal gunboats patrolling the coastline would attack. Few of these residents would ever return. Stagecoach service on the island was halted and the mail boat ceased to run between Matagorda Island and Corpus Christi.

Forshey prepared a map on July 1, 1862, that shows the location of old Fort Washington, the Pass Cavallo Lighthouse, the redoubts below Fort Esperanza, Saluria, and the road from Saluria to Indianola.

On Christmas Day 1862, CSA General John Bankhead Magruder ordered railroad ties and bridges at Indianola de-stroyed to prevent their capture by Federal troops. Further, he ordered his men, "You will burn or destroy the lighthouses at Saluria and Pass Cavallo (the Swash Point light) and all the houses at Pass Cavallo, if practicable . . ."

'Twas easier said than done. The Swash Point Light at Saluria was burned down to the water line, but the Matagorda Island Lighthouse proved to be more formidable. First, the lighting apparatus was removed and concealed. Then, with gunpowder charges the men were able to damage some of the cast-iron plates. Still the tower stood, damaged but not destroyed.

In late November and December 1863, while the island was still under Union control, the lighthouse board officer reported "six sections of the iron tower broken down and nine feet of the foundation blown out laterally." A new lighting ap-paratus for the tower was ordered to replace the one removed and concealed by the Rebels. Clearly the lighthouse board was convinced that the island would remain under Federal control.

However, by March 1864 the 16th Wisconsin was loaded onto five steamers and sixteen sailing vessels and deployed to Louisiana, where they suffered a decisive defeat at Mansfield. The 21st, 22nd, and 23rd Iowa regiments remained on the island to dig a series of redoubts and zig-zag trenches across the island.

By June 15, 1864, the last Union soldier was evacuated from Matagorda Island. The Confederates were able to reoccupy Fort Esperanza until April 9, 1865, when Gen. Robert E. Lee surrendered at Appomattox.

By this time the Matagorda Island Lighthouse tower had become weakened by charges of black powder and cannon shots, and the ever-shifting shoreline was eroding away from under its base.

A three-story temporary tower was fabricated from wood in New Orleans and delivered to the island by mid-summer. On October 15, 1865, the wooden tower was erected, and a fifth-order Fresnel lens was installed and lit.

By 1866 the shell of the iron lighthouse was in danger of toppling. "It is situated about fifty feet from the edge of the beach on a sand formation," a treasury department agent reported. He added that another storm could bring it to "level and total destruction."

A crew was sent from New Orleans to dismantle the iron-plate lighthouse. The ship could not carry the heavy plates as originally planned so they were moved by oxen to a higher and more secure part of the island. According to one account, a narrow gauge rail track was laid. The plates were then loaded into carts placed on the track to be towed by oxen to the tower's new and present-day site. Oral tradition insists that sails were mounted on the carts to ease the load on the oxen. And, perhaps this is true. Certainly many of the island's residents were experienced seamen and shipbuilders.

A seven-meter length of railroad rail was discovered on Matagorda Island during a magnetometer survey conducted in 1978. Nearby was found a "massive wooden timber about 1.5

feet square and part of a large encrusted object." State Marine Archaeologist J. Barto Arnold III concluded that the rail and timber were from a nineteenth-century shipwreck. But could these, in fact, be relics from the lighthouse's removal?

In 1869 the Matagorda Island lightkeeper wrote to the lighthouse board that the makeshift wooden tower "shakes very much during a blow and is considered very insecure." He also noted that his family was crowded, living with the oil butts, table and tools required for the tower and that their living quarters leaked.

By 1870 a new site had been purchased, and in March of 1872 Congress authorized $20,000 to rebuild the Matagorda Island Lighthouse at its new and present-day site, one and a half miles inland.

Finally, on August 19, 1870, a work crew arrived aboard the lighthouse tender *Geranium*. Oxen were again employed to move the remaining plates of the old lighthouse to the new site. But then for a brief time all work was suspended because the deadline had passed for the restoration of Southern lighthouses for which the original $20,000 had been appropriated. In the spring of 1872, Congress approved a special budget item of $20,000 specifically for the Matagorda Island light.

New panels were cast from iron at the Baltimore foundry to replace the panels damaged during the recent conflict. A new third-order Fresnel lens was ordered from Sautter and Company of Paris, France.

At the new site, the tower was assembled on a circular brick foundation. It rose ninety-two feet from the ground from a base that was sixteen feet in diameter. The tower's seven rows of plates are bolted together from the inside along their flanged edges. Each plate is about twelve feet in height and six feet in diameter. Unlike the light at Bolivar Point, there is no brick lining. The spiral staircase inside the tower has 100 steps. The tower was completed by July and was painted flat black.

While rebuilding the Matagorda Lighthouse tower at its new site, the lighthouse board also erected two new Swash

Point Lights in Pass Cavallo, known by locals as the "East and West Shoal Lights." Three years later they would be destroyed by the Storm of 1875. In appearance these Swash Point Lights were identical to the Half Moon Reef Lighthouse that is now on State Highway 35 in Port Lavaca near the Causeway over Lavaca Bay.

Work was suspended again because another $12,000 was needed to complete the Matagorda Island Lighthouse project. This sum was authorized in 1873. Work then began on the keeper's house. The restored tower was lit on the night of Sunday, September 1, 1873.

In 1882 the oil-burning lantern in the Matagorda Island Lighthouse tower was replaced with one fueled with kerosene.

During the Storm of 1886 the tower rocked so violently that one of the bull's eye lenses was shaken from its mounting and shattered on the tower's floor. The water washing over the island rose four feet in the tower, forcing the keeper and the families huddled there to climb even higher.

Storms were not the only danger faced by the lightkeepers. Frequent mention is made of the island's rattlesnakes, which made gardening an undertaking too dangerous to consider. Supplies were purchased from market boats or by sailing to Indianola or Port Lavaca.

In 1956 the light was automated, but Arthur Barr, the light's last keeper, continued to maintain the light until he retired in 1966. His wife, Ruth, is the daughter and granddaughter of the light's two previous keepers, William Heinroth and Theodore O. Olsen. Until recently Arthur and Ruth Barr lived at Port O'Connor. They moved to Ingleside, where Arthur died January 30, 1999.

In 1977 local residents were alarmed when they observed the U.S. Coast Guard removing the lens from the lighthouse to install it at their regional headquarters. In response to public outcry, a compromise was reached. The historic lens was loaned to the Calhoun County Historical Museum, where it can been seen shining through one of the museum's windows, even when the museum is not open. Exhibits include artifacts from Indianola and a diorama depicting the seaport prior to the 1875 storm.

The light in the lighthouse is now powered by batteries that are charged by a solar panel mounted near the top of the lighthouse.

On the island, you can take the shuttle from the dock or hike the two-mile distance to the lighthouse. Visitors are not permitted in the lighthouse but can view a cemetery nearby for the keeper's families.

The Matagorda Island Lighthouse was entered into the National Register of Historic Places in 1974.

An early view of the Matagorda Island Lighthouse at its present-day location. The lightkeeper might be Theodore Olsen or William Heinroth.
— Courtesy of Myrtle Hawes

Known Keepers of the
Matagorda Island Lighthouse

Name	Position	Year Appointed
James Cummings	Keeper	1852
?	?	?
William Chichester	Assistant	1879
Theodore B. Hayes	Assistant	1879
Francis Sinnott	Acting Assistant	1879
Francis Sinnott	Assistant	1881
Robert J. Horton	Acting Assistant	1885
Horace W. Crockett	Acting Keeper	1885
Robert J. Horton	Assistant	1886
Joseph Forrestier	Acting Assistant	1886
Joseph Forrestier	Assistant	1888
Herman Schreiber	Keeper	1888
Joseph Forrestier	Keeper	1889
H. W. Hawes	Acting Assistant	1889
William D. Thompson	Acting Assistant	1896
Edward Reynolds	Assistant	1898
?	?	?
Theodore Olsen	Keeper	1913
William Heinroth	Keeper	1917
Arthur Barr	Keeper	1938

Between 1852 and 1896 the salaries for these positions ranged from a low of $400 per year to a high of $675 per year.

(This list is incomplete because some records are missing.)

Matagorda Island Today

M atagorda Island is an escape from the artificial to the real. Time on the island is not measured on a watch but by the ebb and flow of the tide, the transit of the sun across the daytime sky, the fullness of the moon, and the yap of coyotes at night.

If to everything there is a season and a time for every purpose, Matagorda Island has many seasons.

Today's seaweed and abandoned rope on the beach is tomorrow's dune. Beach morning-glory set abloom in April is replaced by dewberries in May and by late summer, silver-leafed sunflowers.

Sounds on the island are mostly natural, not man-made: the ever-rolling surf, the cheery melody of what sometimes seems to be the world's entire population of meadowlarks, the grunt of an alligator at a water hole.

Black-necked stilts, scarlet tanagers, blue grosbeak, rose-ate spoonbills, piping plovers, brown pelicans, peregrine falcon, and whooping cranes all have their time and place on the island. Experienced birders have logged more than 100 species of birds sighted in a single day on the island during the spring migration. When not overcast, the nighttime sky is free from light pollution, perfect for stargazing.

Hunts are scheduled for deer, feral hog, quail, and dove in season. Flounder are gigged in the shallow waters surrounding the island. Surf fishing is popular along the beach.

There are few native trees, and those few planted by former residents are stunted, twisted by the salt air and wind. Shade shelters and fishing piers are subject to destruction by storms.

Early settlers built cisterns. The U.S. Air Force drilled water wells. The island's ranchers built windmills and stock tanks. All were and are vulnerable to uncertain rainfall and island sand.

A heavy rain can render the roadway to the lighthouse impassable. The island is primitive but not pristine. Partially buried debris at the high tide line bears testimony that mankind has much to learn about living with the Earth. Among the debris have been found messages corked in glass bottles, hard hats, rope, plastic milk cartons, a Civil War-era belt buckle, and a salad dressing bottle with a Japanese label. Trash and treasure alike are relentlessly buried to become the next dune.

There are one hundred steps to the top of the Matagorda Island Lighthouse. This interior view shows how the cast iron plates are bolted together.
— Photo by author

Once the day's hunt has ended, the birds have been sighted, and the island's history retold, nearly all visitors to the island simply sit on the beach and watch the waves roll in and recede.

The island does not take kindly to those who try to make it something that it is not. Visitors treasure the island for its isolation, its primitive, ever-changing nature. Matagorda Island is probably most enjoyed by those who accept the island on its own terms, who pack in their few comforts and pack out their trash, and leave their rigid expectations at home.

The island is not first and foremost a park. It is a wildlife refuge. The great naturalist Aldo Leopold wrote in *Sand County Almanac*, "There are those who can live without wild things and those who cannot." Matagorda Island is for those who cannot.

Before you go, know . . .

Conditions on the island—There is no drinking water on the island. Bring at least one half-gallon per person per day. There is little shade. There are no restaurants, t-shirt shacks, or phones.

Wear comfortable clothing, shoes, and a hat. Swimsuits and shorts will not offer the protection you will want from the sun and wind or the marsh grass if you should choose to stray from one of the island's paths.

The mosquitoes on Matagorda Island can be nonexistent or vicious depending on the rainfall during the previous week. The Karankawas used alligator grease to repel mosquitoes, but you will surely find something less exotic and more effective at your favorite pharmacy.

Getting to the island—There is no roadway to the island. You can take your own boat and tie up to the island's dock, charter a boat, or take the passenger ferry from the Texas Parks and Wildlife Department dock at 16th Street and the Gulf Intracoastal Waterway in Port O'Connor.

Ferry schedule—The ferry fee includes transportation on the island aboard the island's shuttle. Please be aware that schedules and policies change. Call (361) 983-2215 to confirm the schedule, fees, and other details.

On the island—You can bring a bicycle for transportation or "hoof it" if you don't want to rely on the island shuttle. Bicycles and kayaks may be available for rent. It's about a mile and a half across the island from the bayside dock to the gulfside beach. Add another two miles to see the lighthouse.

Special tours—On occasion the Texas Parks and Wildlife Department staff offers a history tour to the lighthouse aboard their shuttle. You will not be allowed to enter the lighthouse. En route you will cross the trenches dug during the Civil War. Other special tour topics include marine biology, birdwatching, and whooping cranes. For schedule, fees, and details phone (361) 983-2215.

Overnight accommodations—Campsites are available on both the beach and on the bay side of the island near the dock. The fee is $4 for each campsite for each four persons. The beach will probably offer you a cooling breeze and more protection from mosquitoes. Don't pitch your tent in the dunes. You might disturb the rattlesnakes there, but they won't bother you on the beach.

Alternatively, there is a four-room bunkhouse that has three to four metal cots in each room for your sleeping bag, a communal living area, kitchen and showers, minimal air-conditioning and heat, for $12 a night. For bunkhouse reservations phone (512) 389-8900.

For your first overnight trip to the island consider taking the last ferry to the island on Saturday to avoid the worst heat of the day. Enjoy the sunset, the stars, and the yap of coyotes at night, then return to the mainland the next morning.

Children—Conditions on the island are probably too rigorous for children under the age of ten unless they are accustomed to wilderness camping. Don't even consider bringing an infant to the island. Most people find that a half day stay is very enjoyable but about all the island adventure that they want.

Lighthouse—You can ride your bike, hike, or take the island shuttle to the Matagorda Island Lighthouse, but you will not be permitted to enter the lighthouse. The salt cedars that lie behind it are a great place to look for warblers during the spring migration, especially if there is a "fall out." (Ask a birder or a park ranger to explain what a "fall out" is.)

Matagorda Island is one of the few places left in Texas where you might see a Texas Horned Lizard. To increase your chances, go to the island during the first week or two in May while they are mating.
— Photo by author

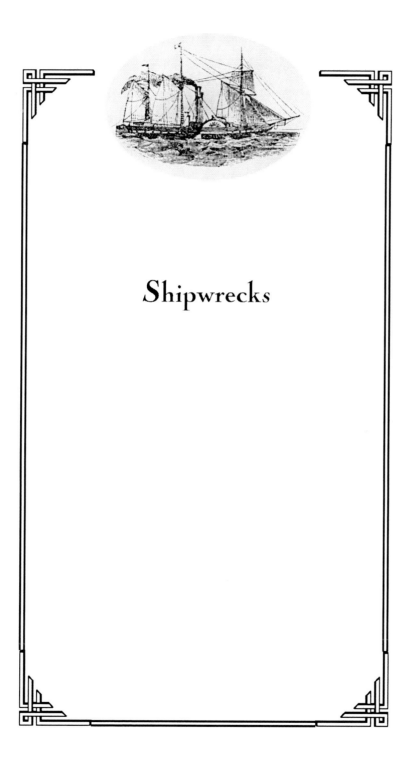

Shipwrecks

To excavate LaSalle's flagship,   La Belle, a cofferdam wall was built around the wreckage site in the twelve-foot deep waters of Matagorda Bay. The water was then pumped out so that the archaeologists could work on the bay bottom. In this photo the outline of the ship can be seen as they work.

— Courtesy Henry Wolff, Jr.

Known Shipwrecks in Matagorda Bay

LaBelle	1685
Balvaneda	1769
Two Friends	1771
El Senor Yedra	1778
Santa Rosa	1815
Thirteen ships (names unknown)	1817
Constitution	1838
Monterey	1848
Envoy	1850
Commercial	1851
William and Mary	1851
William Penn	1851
Perseverance	1853
Unknown	1858
Belvidere	1868
Annie Marie	1869
Comet	1869
Unknown	1869
Elizabeth	1872
Alice	1875
Caroline	1875
Commodore Morbit	1875
Cora Bickford	1875
Delmore	1875
Democrat	1875
Eclipse	1875

Edith Belle NASO	1875
Eleanor	1875
Emory	1875
Flounder	1875
Lake Austin	1875
Maggie	1875
Prouty	1875
Royinia	1875
Sea Gull	1875
Shell Fish	1875
Star of the South	1875
Tidal Wave	1875
Phoenix	1875
Annetta	1875
Josephine	1880
Laurel	1888
Sea Gull	1897
Edna B.	1909
Unknown	1915
Pioneer	1915
Unknown	1935
Illinois	1942
Jan R.	1961
Flossie R. Shaw	1967
Miss Connie	1967

Known Shipwrecks in Pass Cavallo

Unknown	?
Unknown	?
Unknown	?
L'Amiable	1685
Le Superb	1745
Hannah Elizabeth	1835
Pelican	1836
San Felipe	1836
Palmetto	1851
Independence	1852
Meteor	1852
Unknown	1857
Mary Ann	1864
Anna Dale	1865
Lily No. 2	1865
Tom and Able	1872
Peedee	1875
Rescue	1875
Dorio Doria	1885
Quintana	1887
Ada Crossman	1893
Eight barges (names unknown)	1897
Colonel Moore	1927
Sam Houston	1954
SDUB No. 1	1954
Saltdome No. 1	1955
Rose Croix	1961
Miss Hayes	1967

Cemetery Inscriptions

The Old Town Cemetery on Zimmerman Road lies along an old oyster shell ridge. The cemetery and the paved roadway leading to the cemetery are open to the public, but not the privately owned land on either side of the road. Zimmerman Road is an excellent place to look for warblers during the spring migration.

— Photo by author

Old Town Cemetery

(Cemetery on the Ridge)

Information given on marker other than name, birth date and death date is italicized.

Allan, James Chilton, February 13, 1810—November 17, 1851.

Burwell, Frank, June 17, 1869. *Death is certain, the hour unseen.*

Floyd, Col. F.R., *Wife of,* July 23, 1855. *A friend of the poor and servant of the living God, Living was loved, Dying was wept.*

Garner, David, Jr., 1843—1871. *Life's duly done as sinks the day, Light from its load the spirit flies, While heaven and earth combine to say, How blest the righteous when he dies.*

Garner, David, Sr., April 10, 1864. *At the age of 56. We only know that thou hast gone, And that the same return less tide, Which bore thee from us still glides on, And we who mourn thee with it glide.*

Hogan, Denis and William, (no dates). *It is a holy and wholesome thought to pray for the dead that they may be loosed from their sins. Requiescat in Pace.*

Lewis, Amelia D., March 23, 1875—March 29, 1876. *Whom the Gods love, die young.*

Lewis, David, August 20, 1825—August 20, 1886. *Born in East Falmouth Mass. Departed this life by drowning in the great Cyclone. Farewell, O husband dear, farewell. Thou hast left me lonely.*

Lock, Velma Alice, September 23, 1909—September 25, 1973.

Lock, Walter, died June 25, 1907.

Madden, Lydia, July 6, 1839—September 16, 1875. *Died at Indianola. She was a kind and affectionate wife, a fond mother and a friend to all.*

Mahon, Margaret, June 8, 1879. *Wife of Martin Mahon, 55 years. Rest in Peace.*

Mahon, Martin, September 13, 1875. *53 years. Rest in Peace.*

Miller, Ben, March 1857—December 1943. *Aged 87 years, 9 months, 21 days.*

Miller, Bud, 1882—1956.

Miller, Henry, September 14, 1951. *Aged 66 years, 8 months, 28 days.*

Miller, Louise E., April 6, 1859—January 6, 1942. *Mother.*

Miller, Seamon A., 1900-1954.

Nickell, Charles C., *Sgt, U.S. Army, World War II.* May 24, 1920, October 30, 1989.

Pertz, Edward, died December 20, 1914.

Rahtgens, Alice E., May 15, 1830—April 8, 1909. *Born Ireland, Died Port Lavaca, Texas.*

Rahtgens, Henrietta, October 17, 1886. *Aged 30 years. (Panel now missing from marker.)*

Rahtgens, James A., January 8, 1855—October 24, 1858. *Aged 3 years, 9 months and 16 days.*

Rahtgens, James J., born December 1, 1863, died June 20, 1867. *Aged 3 years, 6 months and 19 days.*

Rahtgens, John, March 23, 1886. *Aged 28 years.*

Rahtgens, John H., November 26, 1827—December 8, 1879. *Born in Lubeck, Germany. Aged 52 years, 12 days.*

Rahtgens, Richard, December 15, 1859—December 25. *Aged 10 days.*

Rahtgens, Thomas Henry, 1853—1923.

Rahtgens, William J., August 29, 1866—September 26, 1867. *Aged 1 year 27 days.*

Record, Maybelle, May 1892—May 1914.

Richter, Robert Joseph, December 23, 1932—April 3, 1993. *GM3 U.S. Navy, Korea.*

Umpstead, John P., July 7, 1947—September 5, 1992. *"Imagine That."*

Williams, Anna, wife of A. J. Williams, 1845—1877. *Dear is the spot where Christians sleep, and sweet the strains that Angels pour, O! why should we in anguish weep, They are not lost but gone before.*

Williams, Emily, wife of W. H. Williams, 1840—1866. *We only know that thou hast gone, And that the same return less tide, Which bore thee from us still glides on, And we who mourn thee with it glide.*

Zimmerman Cemetery

*Information given on marker other than name, birth date,
and death date is italicized.*

Barr, Emma K., March 8, 1868—February 5, 1958.

Barr, William D., February 28, 1869—June 24, 1933.

Gonzales, Annie, April 9, 1876—July 20, 1962.

Gonzales, Andrew, December 11, 1876—September 8, 1877.
*Age 8 months, 27 days, Our darling one hath gone before to greet
us on the blissful shore.*

Gonzales, Clarence Henry, February 6, 1904—January 11,
1968.

Gonzales, Frank A., October 19, 1872—died July 16, 1954.

Gonzales, John, April 21, 1838—May 10, 1918. *Aged 80 years,
19 days.*

Gonzales, John D., September 11, 1870—February 25, 1958.

Gonzales, Katherine, December 19, 1843—March 20, 1929.
Aged 85 years, 3 months, 1 day.

Gonzales, Katherine, July 4, 1880-September 23, 1888. *Aged 8
years, 2 months, 18 days. Weep not father and mother for me, For
I am waiting in glory for thee.*

Heinroth, Gunther H., October 8, 1848—January 14, 1920.

Heinroth, Kate Sagner, January 4, 1854—January 25, 1937.

Runge, George H., August 29, 1819—November 1852, *Aged
33.*

Varnell, Priscilla Jane, February 19, 1821—September 7, 1855.

Consort of William M. Varnell, daughter of David and Jane Fluker, born in London, Alabama. Spectator, art thou ready?

Wedig, Georchim, died June 9, 1852.

Wedig, Magdalena F., October 11, 1816—August 15, 1894. *Born at Hildesheun, Germany.*

Wedig, W. Theresa, January 16, 1846—December 29, 1919. *She's gone to worlds above, Where saints and angels meet, To realize our Saviors love, And worship at His feet.*

Wolpers, Conrad, March 10, 1853.

Zimmermann, August G., February 24, 1860—April 9, 1930. *Father. Rest in peace.*

Zimmerman, Dan. G., August 5, 1896—October 24, 1973.

Zimmerman, Elizabeth, June 28, 1874—February 9, 1965.

Zimmerman, Ola, November 25, 1899.

Indianola Cemetery

Information given on marker other than name, birth date, and death date is italicized.

Armstrong, Elmear, November 15, 1841—May 2, 1879. *Wife of George Armstrong. Come unto me all ye who are weary and heavy laden and I will give you rest.*

Armstrong, George, January 28, 1831—November 22, 1885. *Born in Dumfries, Scotland,, died Indianola, Nearer my God to thee, Nearer to thee, Blessed are the pure in heart, For they shall see God.*

Armstrong, James Edward, March 5, 1861—April 28, 1885. *The Lord giveth and the Lord taketh away. Blessed be the name of the Lord.*

Ashworth, William C., August 10, 1857—July 11, 1867. [Original stone had inscription, *I heard the voice of Jesus say, Come unto Me and rest*—according to McCown, 1979.]

Burbank, Charles B., June 25, 1832—January 17, 1876. *Aoue to Resh.*

Clement, (date not visible). *Our Baby, Infant son of P.W. and R. V. Clement.* [*Of such is the King*—according to McCown, 1979.]

Clement, Little Lois, December 16, 1878—died October 12, 1880. *Infant daughter of P. W. and R. V. Clement. Ere sin could blight or sorrow fade, Death came with friendly care, The opening bud to Heaven conveyed, And bade it blossom there.*

Clement, Margaret, January 12, 1846—January 31, 1883.

(Marker now missing.) [*In the Mansion of the Blest*—according to McCown, 1979.]

Clement, *Little Stevie*, December 18, 1869—October 23, 1877. *Son of P. W. and R. V. Clement, Why this cross grieving question, God who took our Idol knew, If our treasure were in Heaven, We would long to follow too.*

Clement, S. C., *no dates.* [Not included in McCown, 1979.]

Coffin, A. W., September 16, 1875. *Aged 32 years.*

Coffin, E. M., January 24, 1869. *Aged 4 years and 9 months, Suffer Little Children to Come Unto Me.*

Coffin, Oscar and Zuileka. *Infants of W. and A. W. Coffin.*

Coffin, Lelia M., May 23, 1821—September 16, 1875. *Wife of Alfred Coffin.*

Collins, James A., July 9, 1867. *Native of Kentucky, departed this life, Aged 31 years.* [Stone broken and patched but upright.]

Collins, Joseph H., February 17, 1867—June 1, 1867. [Lower portion of stone missing, but upright.]

Coutret, Alaniza, 1834—1875. *Born Bern, Switzerland. Died Indianola, Texas.* [Modern marker, not included in McCown, 1979.]

Coutret, Eleanora, 1858-1875. *Born Indianola, Texas. Died Indianola, Texas.* [Modern marker, not included in McCown, 1979.]

Coutret, Joseph, 1809-1875. *Born Paris, France. Died Indianola, Texas 1875.* [Modern marker, not included in McCown, 1979.]

Coutret, Washington, 1852-1875. *Born New Orleans, Louisiana. Died Indianola, Texas.* [Modern marker, not included in McCown, 1979.]

Dahme, Henry, Jr., February 5, 1882. *Aged 32 years.* [*Although dead, Not forgotten*—according to McCown, 1979.]

Dale, Elizabeth Ann, May 22, 1862. *Aged 49 years* died *at Indianola.* [Modern marker, *For her elevated piety & unaffected Christian charity, Her name will be long held in grateful remembrance*—inscription on original marker according to McCown, 1979.]

Demonet, October 20, 1874. *Aged 62 years. Born in Nancy, France.* [Monument is broken, name not clear.]

Dibble, Aug. L., July 4, 1867. *Aged 40 years.*

Dickerson, William, May 14, 1854—April 11, 1873. *Our son,* [Stone broken, laid flat, overgrown with grass, *Brightly beamed lies morn before him, Sweet and holy were earth's ties; but our Father in his wisdom, called him early to the skies*—inscription according to McCown, 1979.]

Franke, Auguste, December 18, 1861—May 31, 1883.

Fromme, Hilmar, February 26, 1860—September 24, 1860.

Fromme, Melanie, February 15, 1858—August 14, 1859. *Suffer little children to come unto me.*

Fuhrmann, August, February 24, 1836—August 3, 1877. *Farewell. Born Baumgarten Schlesingen Germany. Died at Indianola. Aged 41 years and 6 months.*

Grul, Wilheim, February 16, 1834—December 19, 1873. *Ruhe sanft in Kuhlen Grabe, Bis wir einst uns weidersehen.*

Hall, Virginia L., November 29, 1867. *Blessed are the pure in heart for they shall see God. Hope looks beyond the bounds of time when what we now deplore shall rise in full immortal prime and bloom to fade no more.*

Heyck, Valentin, April 7, 1832—September 27, 1876. *Ruhe en Frieden.*

Humphry, J. H., May 29, 1874. *Infant son of J. M. and Sarah Humphrey.* [Marker missing, information from McCown, 1979.]

Hunt, Bennie, March 13, 1866—November 22, 1868.

Iken, Auguste Johanne, July 25, 1867. *Geboren Appmann aus Bremann.* [Only fragments of original stone remain, although there is also a small stone that reads only "A.J.I." and a modern marker that repeats the above information.]

Jacobs, L. H., August 28, 1816—June 1, 1874. [On Simon

marker that has been missing since Easter Sunday 1967—information according to McCown, 1979.]

Jope, Mary Seymour, September 19, 1840—September 16, 1875. *Born in Northumberland County, Virginia, In the way of righteousness is life, and in the pathway thereof.* [Lower portion of stone and remaining inscription is missing. There is also a modern marker that does not include the inscription.]

Keller, Carl, September 6, 1841—June 1871 (year uncertain) [Modern marker, original is missing which had following inscription according to McCown, 1979—*Trennung ist unser Loos, Wiedersehen unser Hoffnung.*]

Kleineke, Henrietta, March 18, 1867. *Consort of Charles Kleineke. Departed this life at Indianola. Aged 31 years. Blessed are they who inherit the Kingdom of Heaven.*

Kleineke, Mary Ella, (No Date). *Daughter of Mary R. And Louis Kleineke, Aged 8 days.* [Marker now missing, original had inscription according to McCown, 1979—*Suffer little children to come unto Me, and forbid them not, for of such is the Kingdom of Heaven.*]

Lang, Christiana, May 31, 1867. *Wife of John H. Lang, Aged 44 years. Rest, Mother, rest, in quiet sleep. While friends in sorrow o'er thee weep, And here their heartfelt offerings bring, And near thy grave thy requiem sing.*

Lang, John, August 24, 1859. *Aged 52 years.* [Stone is very pitted but inscription according to McCown, 1979, read: *Hier ruhst Du, lieber Mann und Vater, befriet von deinen vielen Schmerzen, Die Du hast ausgetanden hier, Nun ruhe sanft in deiner Gruft, Bis des allmaecht'gen Stimme ruft.*]

McCoppin, James, November 23, 1821—July 20, 1883. *Born Liverpool, England. Died, Indianola, Texas. Blessed are the dead that die in the Lord, from henceforth: yea, saith the spirit, that they may rest from their labours, And their works do follow them.*

Marshall, William C., June 24, 1870—died July 1, 1870. *Our littlest Angel.*

Miller, Alexandria, February 2, 1851—February 17, 1858.

Miller, Augusta, April 7, 1865—August 16, 1865.

Moore, D. L., May 17, 1877. *Aged 7 days.*

Moore, Joseph L., died June 14, 1864. *Aged 31 years.*

Moore, Robert B., died September 16, 1875. *Aged 68 years.*

Moore, R. B. Jr., died June 14, 1867. *Aged 12 years.*

Moore, S. C., died January 18, 1879. *Aged 29 years.*

Murdock, Adam, March 15, 1829—October 28, 1869. *Rest in Peace.* [Original stone is now broken and incomplete but there is a separate modern marker.]

Parker, Wm. L., April 2, 1822—July 13, 1867. *Born in Boston.* [There is also a separate modern marker.]

Payne, John W., May 7, 1866. *Aged 12 years and 16 days.*

Payne, Mary Emily, October 6, 1857—July 16, 18__. [Original marker, broken, incomplete, laid flat, but there is also a modern marker, date also not known in McCown, 1979.]

Pearce, August B., August 12, 1857—July 19, 1867.

Pearce, James H., April 3, 1853—July 13, 1867.

Pearce, Louisa, March 27, 1825—July 19, 1867.

Peschke, Anton, November 2, 1826—March 16, 1871. *Geboren in Silesia Preussen, gestorben at Indianola. Pvt. Co. B4 BN Texas Army Confederate States Army.* [Modern marker in addition to original.]

Phillips, John B., June 4, 1810—December 13, 1871. *Aged 61 years, 6 months, 9 days.* [Modern marker.]

Rehner, Auguste, November 12, 1804—February 10, 1879. *Geboren Schulze. Hier ruhet in Gott, unsere gute mutter Schwiemutter & Grossmutter Auguste Rehner Schultze. Gewittmet von ihren trauernden Kindern, Ruhe sanft.*

Runge, Louise, February 4, 1860—September 20, 1860. *Lasset die Kinder zu mir kommen denn Ihrer ist das Himmelreich.*

Schultz, Hannah Rosa, February 3, 1793—October 27, 1875.

We part to meet again. Mother of Dudley Schultz, Born in Prussia. Died at Indianola. Blessed are they that die in the Lord.

Schultz, Sarah H, October 3, 1870. *Daughter of D. and S. Schultz. Aged 10 months. We loved this little lonely one, And would have wished her stay, but let our Father's will be done, she shines in endless day.* [Inscription according to McCown, 1979.]

Seeligson, George, (No Date.) *Blessed are they who die young.*

Seeligson, Kate, (No Date.) *Only daughter of Sophia and Henry Seeligson, aged 18 months. Suffer little children, and forbid them not to come unto me for of such is the Kingdom of Heaven.* [Stone now broken and incomplete.]

Seeligson, Sallie B., December 16, 1874. *Wife of Lewis Seeligson. Died in this city in the 42nd year of her life. The inheritance of the righteous shall be forever.*

Short, C. W., November 17, 1842—May 15, 1884.

Simon, Barbara, April 8, 1857—September 15, 1874. *Tochter van Mathias und Caroline Simon.* [Marker has been missing since Easter Sunday 1967—information from McCown, 1979.]

Simon, Mathias, February 24, 1815—June 24, 1867. *Geboren in Heidelborn, Nassau, Deutchland.* [Marker has been missing since Easter Sunday 1967—information from McCown, 1979.]

Simon, Wilhelmina, April 8, 1866—September 15, 1875. *Tochter von Mathias und Caroline Simon, umgekommen im sturme.* [Marker has been missing since Easter Sunday 1967— information from McCown, 1979.]

Smith, Frank, Herbert, Charley, and Isabel, (No Date.) *Infants of G. D. and R. M. S. Smith. Happy Infants, Early Blest.* [Coffin family marker.]

Steves, Heinrich Gustav, December 6, 1826—July 1867. *Born in Germany. Died in Texas.*

Stiernberg, Wilhelm von, February 9, 1821—October 1, 1865. *Gude Nacht, Fahre voht du traute scele, Mustest frueh von hinnen gehen, Ruhe sanft in dieser grabeshochte, Bis auf einst' ges Wiedersehen.*

Stiernberg, Willie, January 20, 1884—April 17, 1884.

Taylor, Charles, September 20, 1867. *Died in Indianola. Aged 66 years and 6 months.*

Tays, George E., July 9, 1867. *A native of Nova Scotia who departed this life. Aged 37 years.*

Tays, Jemima C. Hichens, July 20, 1867. *A native of Nova Scotia, the beloved wife of the Rev. J. W. Tays. Aged 24 years, a Christian and a mother.*

Tays, Mary Parker, July 16, 1867. *A native of Nova Scotia who departed this life . . .* [This marker is now missing although there is a fragment that reads "27 years." Other information from McCown, 1979.]

Vance, David F., July 17, 1834—July 1, 1867. *Son of Arthur and Janice Vance of Corydon, Indiana, Died at Indianola.* [Stone broken, flat on ground, lower half missing.]

Weisenburg, Florence W., October 19, 1881—December 11, 1883. *Daughter of A. H. and S. F. Weisenberg. Gone but not forgotten.* [Marker missing; information according to McCown, 1979.]

Woodward, Charles Russell, July 17, 1870—April 30, 1871.

Woodward, T. Doddridge, November 16, 1832—October 16, 1865. *Born in Todd County, Kentucky, Rest in Peace.*

Woodward, Emma Parrish, August 17, 1855—October 29, 1858.

Woodward, Proctor, May 13, 1862—July 3, 1867. *Up! Up! Up!*

Woodward, William D., April 15, 1850—July 14, 1852. *Suffer little children, and forbid them not to come unto me for of such is the Kingdom of Heaven.*

Matagorda Island Cemeteries

Lightkeepers Cemetery

Information given on marker other than name, birth date, and death date is italicized.

Forestier, Adeline, March 1—1854, May 13, 1901. *Wife of Joseph Forestier.*

Forestier, Joseph. [No marker but known to be buried here.]

Forestier, William Henry, November 4, 1884—September 1, 1888.

Hawes, Mary Ann Collins—1855-1892.

Olsen, Theodore O., November 16, 1864—December 15, 1918. *Beloved husband of Martha E. Gordy.*

Hawes Markers

Hawes, Forrest C., 1885-1916. [Near U.S. Coast Guard Station closed in 1929.]

Hawes, Hugh Walker, October 21, 1883. *Died at Saluria, Calhoun County, Aged 83 years. Gone but not forgotten.*

Hugh Walker Hawes worked hard to promote Saluria and to develop a port on Matagorda Island, but his dream died when most of the island's residents were forced off the island during the Civil War. Few returned.
— Photo by author

Nichols Cemetery

Nichols, Florence Marian, September 21, 1866—January 10, 1869. *Youngest daughter of Wm. and Adelia P. Nichols. She was lovely, she was fair, And for a while was given, An angel came and claimed his own, And bore her home to heaven.*

Nichols, Cora M., _____ 21, 1830, died April 22, 1849. *Wife of Captain W. Nichols, Woodmen of the World.*

Nichols, *Little* Rose, April 19, 1868. *Sleep on sweet babe, And take thy rest, God called thee home, He thought it best.*

Nichols, *Little* Kate, July 27, 1865—July 31, 1865. *Sleep, sweet Angel, We all hope to meet you.*

Wildflower
and
Birding Lists

Beach Evening Primrose (Oenothera drummondii) *can be seen in bloom on Matagorda Island from March to sometimes as late as December.*

— Photo by author

Wildflowers

Following is a list of forty wildflowers commonly seen in the area of Magnolia Beach, between the Old Town and Indianola cemeteries, and on Matagorda Island. On any given weekend between March 1 and November 30 you should readily find at least a dozen or more wildflowers in bloom by referring to this chart and a good field guide.

Generally in bloom = ▨   Not in bloom = ☐

Common Name	J	F	M	A	M	J	J	A	S	O	N	D
Alamo Vine				▨	▨	▨	▨	▨	▨	▨	▨	
Alophia			▨	▨	▨							
Blue Curls			▨	▨	▨							
Bluebonnets			▨	▨	▨							
Blue-Eyed Grass		▨	▨									
Brown-Eyed Susan					▨	▨	▨					
Coast Germander			▨	▨				▨	▨	▨	▨	▨
Coast Mistflower					▨	▨	▨	▨	▨	▨	▨	▨
Coral Bean			▨	▨	▨	▨						
Day flower			▨	▨	▨	▨	▨	▨	▨	▨	▨	
Dewberries			▨	▨	▨							
Fringed Paccoon			▨	▨								
Gaura		▨	▨						▨	▨	▨	
Goat-foot Morning Glory					▨	▨	▨	▨	▨			
Greenthread		▨	▨	▨	▨							
Indian Blanket		▨	▨	▨	▨	▨	▨	▨	▨	▨	▨	▨
Indian Paintbrush			▨	▨	▨	▨						

Common Name	J	F	M	A	M	J	J	A	S	O	N	D
Lantana			X	X	X	X	X	X	X	X	X	X
Meadow Pink		X	X	X	X							
Mexican Hat					X	X	X	X	X	X		
Mexican Petunia			X	X	X	X	X	X	X	X		
Missouri Primrose			X	X	X	X	X					
Pink Mint		X	X	X	X							
Prickly Pear			X	X	X	X						
Prickly Poppy		X	X	X	X	X	X	X	X	X	X	
Rain Lily				X	X							
Scarlet Pimpernel			X	X	X							
Sea Lavender					X	X	X	X	X	X	X	X
Seacoast Goldenrod								X	X	X		
Sensitive Briar				X	X	X	X	X				
Showy Pink Primrose		X	X	X	X							
Silver-leafed Sunflower						X	X	X	X	X		
Spanish Dagger	X	X	X	X								
Spider Lily		X	X	X								
Spiderwort		X	X	X	X							
Square-bud Day Primrose			X	X	X	X	X	X	X	X	X	
Stiff-Stemmed Flax		X	X	X	X	X						
Texas Thistle		X	X	X	X	X						
Texas Vervain		X	X	X	X	X	X	X	X	X	X	X
Turk's Cap		X	X	X	X	X	X	X	X	X	X	X

Calhoun County Birding

More bird species have been reported in Calhoun County during the North America Migratory Bird Count held in May *than any other county in the entire nation*. Calhoun County has held this record since 1991, when the count began even though the peak period for migration is more typically the second or third week in April. Two hundred and twenty-eight species were reported during the 1997 count.

Eight of the ninety-five birding sites on the Great Texas Coastal Birding Trail are located in Calhoun County (#16 plus 30 through 36). And this doesn't include the Aransas National Wildlife Refuge (#37) that overlaps portions of Calhoun, Aransas, and Refugio counties.

Is there a birder in Texas who doesn't know the Aransas NWR is the home of the nation's only wild and migrating flock of whooping cranes? The first of the cranes arrive about November 11 and most have selected their territory at Aransas by January. In April they will depart again to fly north to the Wood Buffalo Park of Canada's Northwest Territories.

There is an observation tower at the refuge with a scope, but the best way to see the cranes is to enter their marshy realm by boat. Capt. Robbie Gregory offers birding tours aboard his catamaran to the saltwater marshes of Welder Flats and the Aransas NWR while there are whoopers there to see. Gregory departs from a dock at Port O'Connor so that he is able to get birders to the whoopers quicker than other boats.

While the whoopers are at their nesting grounds in

Canada, Gregory will take birders to Bird Island, a spoil island rookery in Pass Cavallo where birders can observe nesting Roseate Spoonbills, Tri-colored Herons and Reddish Egrets through binoculars or a scope from the boat. For details phone (361) 983-2862.

Whitmire Division of the Aransas National Wildlife Refuge

When the Aransas National Wildlife Refuge acquired about 3,000 acres of land near Powderhorn Lake, refuge manager Brent Giezentanner asked Mrs. Doris Wyman of Port Lavaca to compile a year-round list of birds for the new acquisition that is now known as the Myrtle Foester Whitmire Division of the Aransas National Wildlife Refuge.

The Whitmire Unit is not open to the public because the access road to the refuge crosses privately owned property. In past years, the land owner has graciously allowed access during the Annual Birding Classic competition in April. Phone the refuge at (361) 286-3539 for details.

Matagorda Island
State Park

A nother option is to bird Matagorda Island, which is man-
aged as a state park and as a unit of the Aransas National
Wildlife Refuge System. For the best birding, go over on the
last ferry of the day from Port O'Connor and return the next
day so that you are on the island while the birds are most
active.

(For more details read the chapter entitled "Matagorda
Island Today" including the "Before You Go" section.)

A free birding list for the 317 species recorded on Matagorda Island is available at the Texas Parks and Wildlife office
where you will board the ferry to the island (16th Street and
the Intracoastal Waterway).

*Whooping Cranes return to the Aransas National Wildlife Refuge each
year beginning about November 10. In January the first of the whoopers begin to depart with the last of them generally leaving in April.*
— Courtesy U.S. Fish and Wildlife Service

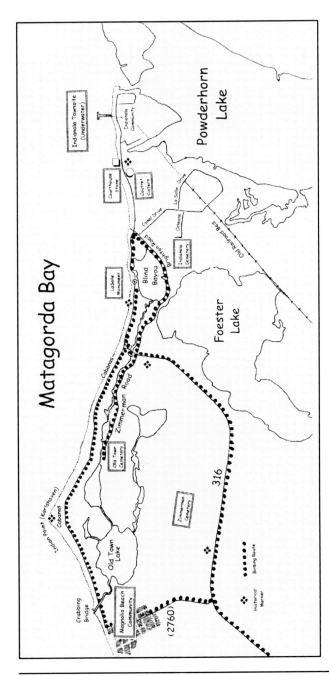

Shown is the birding route used by Doris Wyman for her weekly survey. Note also the locations of the Old Town and Indianola cemeteries. The "no trespass" sign at the entrance to Zimmerman Road refers to the privately owned land on either side of the roadway. The cemetery and the paved roadway are open to the public.

— Map by author

Old Town-Indianola Birding List

(Magnolia Beach to Indianola)

A birding route established by Doris Wyman of Port Lavaca is known by locals as "Magic Road," although you won't see any sign posts bearing that name. (See map on previous page.)

Not Likely =	Maybe =	Good Chance =	Very likely =

Species	J	F	M	A	M	J	J	A	S	O	N	D
Common Loon												
Pied-billed Grebe												
Horned Grebe												
Eared Grebe												
American White Pelican												
Brown Pelican												
Double-crested Cormorant												
Neo-tropic Cormorant												
Anhinga												
Magnificent Frigatebird												
American Bittern												
Least Bittern												
Great Blue Heron												
Great Egret												
Snowy Egret												
Little Blue Heron												

Species	J	F	M	A	M	J	J	A	S	O	N	D
Tri-colored Heron												
Reddish Egret												
Cattle Egret												
Green-backed Heron												
Black-crowned Night Heron												
Yellow-crowned Night Heron												
White Ibis												
White-faced Ibis												
Glossy Ibis												
Roseate Spoonbill												
Wood Stork												
Fulvous Whistling Duck												
Black-bellied Whistling Duck												
Greater White-fronted Goose												
Snow Goose												
Ross' Goose												
Canada Goose												
Green-winged Teal												
Mottled Duck												
Mallard												
Northern Pintail												
Blue-winged Teal												
Cinnamon Teal												
Northern Shoveler												
Gadwall												

Species	J	F	M	A	M	J	J	A	S	O	N	D
American Wigeon												
Canvasback												
Redhead												
Ring-necked Duck												
Greater Scaup												
Lesser Scaup												
Surf Scoter												
Common Goldeneye												
Bufflehead												
Hooded Merganser												
Common Merganser												
Red-breasted Merganser												
Ruddy Duck												
Black Vulture												
Turkey Vulture												
Osprey												
American Swallow-tailed Kite												
Black-shouldered Kite												
Mississippi Kite												
Northern Harrier												
Sharp-shinned Hawk												
Cooper's Hawk												
Harris' Hawk												
Red-shouldered Hawk												
Broad-winged Hawk												

Species	J	F	M	A	M	J	J	A	S	O	N	D
Swainson's Hawk												
White-tailed Hawk												
Red-tailed Hawk												
Crested Caracara												
American Kestrel												
Merlin												
Peregrine Falcon												
Northern Bobwhite												
Yellow Rail												
Black Rail												
Clapper Rail												
King Rail												
Virginia Rail												
Sora												
Purple Gallinule												
Common Moorhen												
American Coot												
Sandhill Crane												
Black-bellied Plover												
Lesser Golden Plover												
Snowy Plover												
Wilson's Plover												
Semipalmated Plover												
Killdeer												
Mountain Plover												

Species	J	F	M	A	M	J	J	A	S	O	N	D
American Oyster Catcher												
Black-necked Stilt												
American Avocet												
Greater Yellowlegs												
Lesser Yellowlegs												
Solitary Sandpiper												
Willet												
Spotted Sandpiper												
Upland Sandpiper												
Whimbrel												
Long-billed Curlew												
Hudsonian Godwit												
Marbled Godwit												
Ruddy Turnstone												
Sanderling												
Semi-palmated Sandpiper												
Western Sandpiper												
Least Sandpiper												
White-rumped Sandpiper												
Baird's Sandpiper												
Pectoral Sandpiper												
Dunlin												
Stilt Sandpiper												
Buff-breasted Sandpiper												
Short-billed Dowitcher												

Species	J	F	M	A	M	J	J	A	S	O	N	D
Long-billed Dowitcher												
Common Snipe												
Wilson's Phalarope												
Laughing Gull												
Franklin's Gull												
Bonaparte's Gull												
Ring-billed Gull												
Herring Gull												
Gull-billed Tern												
Caspian Tern												
Royal Tern												
Sandwich Tern												
Forster's Tern												
Least Tern												
Black Tern												
Black Skimmer												
White-winged Dove												
Mourning Dove												
Inca Dove												
Common Ground Dove												
Black-billed Cuckoo												
Yellow-billed Cuckoo												
Groove-billed Ani												
Barn Owl												
Great-Horned Owl												

Species	J	F	M	A	M	J	J	A	S	O	N	D
Lesser Nighthawk												
Common Nighthawk												
Chimney Swift												
Ruby-throated Hummingbird												
Black-chinned Hummingbird												
Belted Kingfisher												
Red-headed Woodpecker												
Yellow-bellied Sapsucker												
Olive-sided Flycatcher												
Eastern Wood Peewee												
Yellow-bellied Flycatcher												
Acadian Flycatcher												
Willow Flycatcher												
Least Flycatcher												
Eastern Phoebe												
Vermillion Flycatcher												
Great Crested Flycatcher												
Brown-crested Flycatcher												
Western Kingbird												
Eastern Kingbird												
Scissor-tailed Flycatcher												
Horned Lark												
Purple Martin												
Tree Swallow												
Northern Rough-winged Swallow												

Species	J	F	M	A	M	J	J	A	S	O	N	D
Bank Swallow												
Cliff Swallow												
Barn Swallow												
Bewick's Wren												
House Wren												
Winter Wren												
Sedge Wren												
Marsh Wren												
Ruby-crowned Kinglet												
Blue-gray Gnatcatcher												
Veery												
Hermit Thrush												
Wood Thrush												
American Robin												
Gray Catbird												
Northern Mockingbird												
Brown Thrasher												
Long-billed Thrasher												
Curve-billed Thrasher												
American Pipit												
Cedar Waxwing												
Loggerhead Shrike												
European Starling												
White-eyed Vireo												
Solitary Vireo												

Species	J	F	M	A	M	J	J	A	S	O	N	D
Yellow-throated Vireo												
Warbling Vireo												
Philadelphia Vireo												
Red-eyed Vireo												
Blue-winged Warbler												
Golden-winged Warbler												
Tennessee Warbler												
Orange-crowned Warbler												
Nashville Warbler												
Northern Parula												
Yellow Warbler												
Chestnut-sided Warbler												
Magnolia Warbler												
Yellow-rumped Warbler												
Black-throated Green Warbler												
Blackburnian Warbler												
Yellow-throated Warbler												
Palm Warbler												
Bay-breasted Warbler												
Blackpoll Warbler												
Cerulean Warbler												
Black and White Warbler												
American Redstart												
Prothonotary Warbler												
Worm-eating Warbler												

Species	J	F	M	A	M	J	J	A	S	O	N	D
Northern Waterthrush												
Connecticut Warbler												
Mourning Warbler												
Common Yellowthroat												
Hooded Warbler												
Wilson's Warbler												
Canada Warbler												
Yellow-breasted Chat												
Summer Tanager												
Scarlet Tanager												
Northern Cardinal												
Pyrrhuloxia												
Rose-breasted Grosbeak												
Blue Grosbeak												
Indigo Bunting												
Painted Bunting												
Dickcissel												
Green-tailed Towhee												
Rufous-sided Towhee												
Bachman's Sparrow												
Cassin's Sparrow												
Chipping Sparrow												
Field Sparrow												
Vesper Sparrow												
Lark Sparrow												

Species	J	F	M	A	M	J	J	A	S	O	N	D
Savannah Sparrow	■	■	■		◨				◨	■	■	■
Grasshopper Sparrow												
Sharp-tailed Sparrow				◨						◨		
Seaside Sparow												
Lincoln's Sparrow				◨					◨			
Swamp Sparrow	■	■	■									
White-throated Sparrow					◨				◨	■	■	■
White-crowned Sparrow					◨				◨			
Dark-eyed Junco				◨						◨		
Red-winged Blackbird	■	■	■	■	■	■	■	■	■	■	■	■
Eastern Meadowlark	■	■	■	■	■	■	■	■	■	■	■	■
Western Meadowlark				◨	◨					◨		
Yellow-headed Blackbird		◨		◨					◨			
Brewer's Blackbird				◨					◨			
Great-tailed Grackle	■	■	■	■	■	■	■	■	■	■	■	■
Boat-tailed Grackle		◨							◨			
Common Grackle	■									■	■	■
Bronzed Cowbird												
Brown-headed Cowbird	■	■	■	■					■	■	■	■
Orchard Oriole								▮				
Northern Oriole				■					■			
American Goldfinch	■	■	■		◨				◨	■		
House Sparrow	■	■	■	■	■	■	■	■	■	■	■	■

265 Species

Bibliography

For those who would like to know more about Indianola, Brownson Malsch's *Indianola, Mother of West Texas* is probably the best single source of information. Other sources used for this book include:

Arnold III, J. Barto. *A Matagorda Bay Magnetometer Survey and Site Test Excavation Project.* Austin: Texas Antiquities Committee, Publication No. 9, 1982.

Baker, T. Lindsay. *Lighthouses of Texas.* College Station: Texas A&M University Press, 1991.

Dworaczyk, Rev. Edward. *The first Polish Colonies of America in Texas.* San Antonio, Texas: The Naylor Co., 1979.

Emmett, Chris. *Shanghai Pierce, A Fair Likeness.* Norman, Oklahoma: University of Oklahoma Press, 1953.

———. *Texas Camel Tales.* Austin: Steck-Vaughn Company, 1969, edited reprint of 1932 original.

Ficklen, Lonnie, Frances Hartzog, Marion Rhodes, Betty Stevenson, Eula Grace Wedig. *Indianola Memories.* Calhoun County: Indianola Pilgrimage Committee for Calhoun County Sesquicentennial, 1986.

Fornell, Earl Wesley. *The Galveston Era: Texas Crescent on the Eve of Secession.* Austin: University of Texas Press, 1961.

French, George. *Indianola Scrapbook.* Austin: Jenkins Publishing Co., San Felipe Press, 1974 reprint of original with index compiled by Leonard Joe McCown, Calhoun County Historical Survey Committee.

Guthrie, Keith. *Texas Forgotten Ports: Mid-Gulf Ports from Corpus Christi to Matagorda Bay.* Austin: Eakin Press, 1988.

Grimes, Roy. *300 Years in Victoria County.* Victoria: Victoria Advocate Publishing Co., 1985.

Hauschild, Henry J. *The Runge Chronicle, a German Saga of Success.* Austin: The Whitley Company, April 1990.

Jackson, Jack. *Lost Cause, The Taylor Sutton Feud and Reconstruction Texas.* North Hampton, Massachusetts: Kitchen Sink Press, 1998.

Karnei, Shirley A., and Frances Hartman, co-editors. *Yorktown, Texas 150 Year Anniversary.* Yorktown Historical Society. Yorktown: The Printery, 1997.

Kellogg, C. F., notes written in his copy of *The History of the 21st Iowa,* in the 1890s. Book is now in Iowa State Historical Library.

Krueger, Max Amadeus Paulus. *Second Fatherland, The Life and Fortunes of a German Immigrant.* College Station and London: Texas A&M University Press, 1976.

Malsch, Brownson. *Indianola: Mother of West Texas.* Austin: Shoal Creek Publishers, Inc., 1977.

McAlister, Wayne H. and Martha K. *Matagorda Island, A Naturalist's Guide.* Austin: University of Texas Press, 1993.

McCown, Leonard Joe, *Cemeteries of Indianola.* Privately printed by Leonard Joe McCown in 1979.

Oppenheimer, Evelyn. *Gilbert Onderdonk: The Nurseryman of Mission Valley, Pioneer Horticulturist.* Denton: University of North Texas Press, 1991.

Pioneer Flour Mills. *100th Anniversary Pioneer Flour Mills, San Antonio, Texas, 1851-1951, A Scrapbook of pictures and events in San Antonio during the last 100 years.* San Antonio: The Naylor Company, 1951.

Rhodes, George Fred. *Historically Speaking,* a series of newspaper articles that appeared in the *Port Lavaca Wave* between 1985 and 1989.

Sheppard, Lorna Geer. *An Editor's View of Early Texas in the Days of the Republic as Depicted in The Northern Standard (1842-1846).* Austin: Eakin Press, 1998.

Spurlin, Charles D., editor. *The Civil War Diary of Charles A. Leuschner.* Austin: Nortex Press, an imprint of Sunbelt Media, Inc., 1992.

Stevers, Rex H. *Handling the Mails at Corpus Christi.* Dallas: Taylor Publishing Co., 1997.

Tyler, Ron, editor in chief. *The New Handbook of Texas.* 6 Vols. Austin: The Texas State Historical Association, 1996.

Waugh, Juliet Nott. *Castroville and Henri Castro, Empressario.* 1966 reprint of 1934 original. Castroville: Castro Colonies Heritage Association, 1966.

Weaver, Bobby D. *Castro's Colony, Empressario Development in Texas, 1842-1865.* College Station: Texas A&M Press, 1985.

Young, Kevin R. *To the Tyrants Never Yield, A Texas Civil War Sampler.* Plano: Wordware Publishing Inc., Regional Division, Plano, Texas, 1992.

About the Author

LINDA WOLFF moved to Port Lavaca in 1983 to become staff writer and bureau chief for the *Victoria Advocate* newspaper. She began re - search for this book after hearing tales of the great Indianola storms and visiting Matagorda Island.

Between 1986 and 1991 she sponsored a series of Mata - gorda Island Adventures, an annual excursion to the island. At the time there was no ferry to the island and it was only acces- sible by boat. The annual excursions included birding and wildflower field trips, history tours to the Matagorda Island Lighthouse, and a LaSalle feast.

In 1991 she ended the Adventures to the Island after con- vincing the Texas Parks and Wildlife Department to establish a public passenger ferry to the island. She then focused more of her attention on Indianola.

By this time her friendship with naturalists Dr. Wayne McAlister and his wife, Martha, had led her to record the wild- flower species at Indianola and to persuade Doris Wyman to conduct a weekly birding survey.

In 1993 she left the *Victoria Advocate* and accepted a posi- tion as consultant to Texas Parks and Wildlife Department as staff support for the Governor's Task Force on Nature Tourism.

In 1994 she had an opportunity to ride a camel for two days between Brackettville and Del Rio with Howdy Fowler

and his family as they were retracing Beale's route from Indi -
anola to California.

Today she is employed by Golden Crescent Regional Planning
Commission as the environmental resources coordinator and is
working with Texas Settlement–Independence Region, a coalition
of seventeen counties, to develop the area's heritage tourism.

Wolff also publishes and edits a website about Indianola and
Matagorda Island, at www.indianolabulletin.com.

Inaugurating the ferry, 1991.
— Photo by Bobby Tomek

Camel ride to Del Rio, 1994.
— Photo by Yahouskin Fowler

Index

Comal Springs, 13
Comanches, 7-8, 17
Comfort, 33
Concho Expedition Company, 32
Confederate Army, 44-46, 47, 49-52, 95
Confederate Congress, 45
Convoy, 6
Cook, William M., 14, 19
Cooke, Col. L. P., 15-16
Cooper, E. K., 30, 85, 92
Copano Bay, 16, 81
Corpus Christi, 50, 57
Cortinas, Juan, 41
Court, ———, 90
Coutret, Alois, 67
Cox, Jim, 60, 64
Crescent team, 61
Cristman, John W., 64
Crockett, Horace W., 100
Crosand, D. E., 45
Crosby, Claude, 67
Cuero, 4, 55, 62, 63, 69, 71
Cuero Land and Immigration Company, 63
Cummings, James, 32, 84, 85, 86, 93, 100
Cunningham, Solomon G., 24

~D~

Dahme's Corner, 73
Daniel Webster, 37
Davage, R. A., 87
Davidson, James, 60
Davis, Edmund J., 58, 60, 63
    Jefferson, 3
Day, Alf, 63
Decrow's Point, 10, 17, 29
Delta, 29
Democratic Telegraph and Texas Register, 22
Denmark, 13
Dennison, J. W., 83
Department of Texas, 43
DeWitt County, 58, 62
d'Orvanne, Bourgeois, 11

Donaldson's place, 21
Dove, Andrew, 57
Dresel, Gustav, 22
Dubois, L., 88
Duke, Thomas M., 84, 87
Duncan, James H., 40
Dunohoe, Jonathan, 87

~E~

East and West Shoal Lights, 98
Eberly, Angelina Belle Peyton, 17, 24, 25
Ebro, 9
Eckhardt, Caesar, 21
    Charles, 9, 20, 21
Eclipse, 73
Edward & Belden, 83
8th Military District, 41
El Paso, 22, 26
El Paso Railroad, 61
El Paso road, 45
Ellin, William, 88
Ellis, Martha, 68
emancipation, 52
England, Daniel, 87
Envoy, 26
Episcopal Church of the Ascension, 60, 61
Ernst, Fredrich, 7
Ervendberg, Rev. Louis, 13
European, 19
Evergreen Cemetery, 65
Everhard, 14
Evers, B., 53
Excel, 6
Excelsior team, 61

~F~

Falls City, 36
Farwell, ———, 90
Fashion, 35, 87
Ferdinand, 12
Ferguson and Harrel, 8, 91
Fey, Pius, 63
Finlay, George P., 47
Fischer, Dr., 68